About Courtship

Relationship Principles for Adventists

Shanley Lutchman

ALTARIAH BOOKS LTD.

About Courtship—Relationship Principles for Adventists

Shanley Lutchman

Cover design and interior by Megan Kruger from Firefli Design Studio.

Printed in South Africa by Altariah Books Ltd.

ISBN 978-0-620-64639-0

For additional copies visit
www.shanleylutchman.com/books

Contents

Preface

"He that watereth shall be watered also himself."
Proverbs 11:25

When God gives you something, you have an obligation to share it with others. My interest in the subject of courtship placed me on a journey of discovery and learning. God has been my Guide on that journey. It started out as an insignificant fascination. It developed into a deep desire to please God and to know how best to give Him glory in this area of my life. I do not know why God decided to take me on this journey. He could have left me in my ignorance to do things the way that they have always been done. I am grateful that He did not leave me and I feel indebted to those who have not yet learned what I have learned on this journey.

I wrote this book because I could not quiet the urgings of the Holy Spirit to write and to publish what I have learned about courtship. Even the process of writing has been a learning experience. I admit that I am not highly experienced in this area. I have drawn my conclusions mostly from Inspiration and from the experiences of others. What I have written in the book is what I believe to be true and the way I intend to go about relationships. What I have written here is what I wish that 15-year-old Shanley knew. My single desire is that you may be blessed by this book.

Acknowledgements

"Firstly, I thank my God through Jesus Christ for you all"
Romans 1:8

I am thankful to a number of individuals who helped me to create this book. I am immensely grateful to my dearest friend and brother in Christ, Peter Pietrie for his deep love for Christ and passion for the well-being of young people. This has been a source of motivation in completing this book. I would like to thank Chris Chinonge for his knowledge and insight in assisting me to refine some key concepts presented in the book. Sasha Langford and Palesa Motjuwadi, your contributions were invaluable.

Also, I would like to acknowledge the many people who have provided feedback in reviewing earlier drafts of this book. Among these are Lisette Morgan, Dr Randy Siebold, Dr Paul Charles, and Lindelinkosi Nyoni.

Last, and most importantly, I would like to thank God, my Master, my Father, my Friend, my ever-present Companion, my Help in the time of trouble, my Defender, my Shield, my Strength. All glory to a faithful God. If your life is touched by this book, then all the credit it due to God, the Creator and Lord of all the worlds.

Introduction

"*The path of the righteous is like the morning sun, shining ever brighter till the full light of day.*"

Proverbs 4:18 (NIV)

Introduction

In my first year at university there was a girl that I was interested in. She was Adventist. Baptized. Beautiful. Intelligent. And she seemed to be an answer to prayer. She was everything that I wanted in a girl. She was the one I believed that God wanted for me. After a few unsuccessful attempts at getting her to go on a date with me, I realized that it wasn't going to happen. It took me over a year to come to this conclusion—yes, she was that impressive!

At the end of my second year, God showed me clearly from His Word that it was not His intention for me to be in a relationship at that point in my life—there were things that He needed me to learn first. I then made the decision to stay single until God showed me otherwise. This decision allowed me to experience a great amount of spiritual growth and mental development. I will forever cherish that day that God clearly showed me what He wanted me to do.

During those single days I came across God's plan for courtship—the way that He wants young people to enter into relationships and get married. I may never have found this plan if I had not followed God's direction to remain single for as long as it was His will for my life. It is this plan that I would like to share with you in this book. I hope that in the pages of this book you may find a blessing and also get a better understanding of what God desires for your life. I have been greatly blessed by what God showed me, and I hope that you may also be blessed as I show it to you.

Purpose of this book

There are a few things that I hope you gain from reading this book. Firstly, I would like to make you aware of the courtship procedure that was followed by God's people in Bible times. This procedure was not based on the culture of the Bible characters or the norms of the times in which they lived. It was the way the righteous people of God went about getting married, and they did it this way because it was in line with the principles upon which the Kingdom of God is built.

The courtship procedure is also the way that our Adventist pioneers went about getting married. The book *Messages to Young People* is a book rich with principles about relationships. But as you learn about the courtship procedure, you will find that a lot of what you have read in the Spirit of Prophecy books about relationships will make much more sense. The courtship procedure appears to fit the principles in the Spirit of Prophecy books much like a hand fits into a glove.

The divorce rate in the church is slowly approaching the divorce rate outside of the church. This is because we do marriage inside the church in the same way that marriage is done outside of the church. If we can go back to doing things according to the principles of God we can reduce and even eliminate divorce in the church. I do not want you to get divorced one day. I want you to have a successful marriage. For your own benefit, for the benefit of your children, for the benefit of the church, for the benefit of the community in which you live and for the benefit of the entire world.

Up to now, most of what you know about getting into relationships and getting married has come from what you have seen your parents, family and friends do, what you have seen in movies, read in books, or watched on TV and collected from other non-Christian and non-Adventist sources. In this book I would like to inform you from the Word of God and from the Spirit of Prophecy how God would have you go about getting married. In doing this, I hope to add to your happiness and to protect you from being hurt by relationships, especially if you are a young lady.

I've noticed that there are a lot of young, attractive girls in the church of God today. Praise God! He has really blessed this church with beautiful girls. I often find that it is just these young ladies that get taken by smooth-talking, ladies-man type of guys who don't have intentions of getting married and establishing and bringing up a family in the fear of the Lord. No, they just want to play around. Have some fun. And they don't care about the emotional ruin that they cause on the young ladies. So if you are a young lady, I hope that this book will equip you to avoid being led astray by young men whom Satan places in your life to ruin you spiritually and emotionally. I hope that you will one day marry a godly young man, who will lead you and your future children to become true citizens of God's Kingdom.

For the young men reading this book, my desire is that you may become the heads of the home that God desires you to become; that you may know

> *True fulfilment in life is not found in a relationship with another human being; it is found in a relationship with Jesus.*

how to treat young ladies the way that God would have you treat them; that you may become a man by God's definition of a man. As a young boy I was often teased for not being like other boys when it came to chatting up girls. Looking back on it, it was not necessary for me to be a flirt, smooth-talking or a player-type. Building and cherishing friendships with girls was all that was needed during those days. However, I didn't know what the principles of courtship were, and so it caused a lot of frustration. I thought I was supposed to be like the other guys. I wish I had a book like this one!

For both young men and young women, I hope that in reading this book you will become happy as a single person and that you will enjoy being single. If you can be happy as a single person, you will be happy as a married person. The word is "contentment". If you are content to be single, you will be content when you are married. As a single person you may think "If I can find the right person to marry, then I will be happy", but happiness does not come from a relationship with another human being. And you will only be happy in a relationship if you are happy as a single person. If you try to find happiness in a relationship and you do get married, after a few years of marriage you may then say "If only I had children, then I would be happy." And later on, "If only I had some grandchildren, then I would be happy." And so on. You don't need a change of circumstances; you need to learn to be content.

True fulfilment in life is not found in a relationship with another human being; it is found in a relationship with Jesus. Part of this involves discovering your skills and talents and using them to the glory and honour of God. I hope to show you how you may do this.

There are examples of single men and women in the Bible who did great things for God: Elijah, Jeremiah, Paul, Miriam. This may be God's will for you too. You may say "Well, I'm lonely" but behind every experience in life God has a reason:

> Your feelings of unrest and homesickness or loneliness may be for your good. Your heavenly Father means to teach you to find in Him the friendship and love and consolation that will satisfy your most earnest

hopes and desires.

Our High Calling pg. 64

Once again, fulfilment in life is found only in God. If you are content being single, you will be content when you are married. If you are not yet content being single, you probably are not ready to be married yet. By reading this book, I hope that you will become content as a single person so that you will be ready for marriage if you do choose to get married and if the Lord desires marriage for you.

Dating vs. Courting

Dating and courting are sometimes used to describe the same situation of being in a one-on-one relationship with someone of the opposite sex. In this book I use the two words to describe two totally different methods of finding a life-partner. A dating relationship is a relationship that is really just about having a good time together—social entertainment. In dating, marriage is not always the goal. Couples may date for many months or years without planning to get married. Sometimes in a dating relationship, the lady may want to settle down and get married but the guy has no intentions of proposing. He's just having a good time. So the relationship may keep dragging on and on with no real purpose other than having a good time together.

Courtship, on the other hand, is a relationship that is focussed on evaluating the character of the person you are courting. And the reason you are doing this is because you are trying to find out if this person will be a suitable match for you as a life-partner. While you are courting someone, you are constantly asking yourself "Is this person the one that I should marry?" If the person is not a good match for you, you end the courtship and you look for someone else. If the person is a good match for you, then you get married. Dating and courting may seem similar on the outside, but they are different, and you will see just how different they are as you read this book.

The Courtship Procedure

Is it possible for there to be a courtship procedure? Don't things happen naturally? Don't you just go with the flow, and see where it goes? Yes, you may feel that way. I felt that way too when I came across the courtship procedure. But what I found is that the common way of dating is also a procedure. The only reason it doesn't feel like a procedure is because we are so used to it. We have seen it happen so many times in movies, books, and in the lives of those around us that we don't think of it as a procedure. We think of it as the natural way that things are to take place. But it is not the natural way. It is a procedure, set up by Satan to destroy the relationship experience of Christians. Here is the dating procedure:

1. Boy and Girl meet, and they like each other
2. Boy asks Girl on a date
3. Boy and Girl date often, physical affection is accepted
4. Boy and Girl decide to inform their parents
5. Eventually, if Girl is lucky, Boy will ask Girl to marry him
6. Boy and Girl marry and live happily ever after

See, it's a procedure. But it has many flaws. And you will see the flaws in this dating procedure as I show you the Biblical principles of courtship and the courtship procedure. The courtship procedure in this book may go against what you consider the "natural way" that things should unfold. But at one time it was the common, natural way of starting a marriage relationship. The dating procedure is the cause of the many broken relationships, the luke-warmness, and the broken hearts that we find in the church today. It is also one of the reasons why we are still on earth and have not finished the work that Jesus left for us to do.

Unlike the dating procedure, the courtship procedure is based on the principles of God's Kingdom. The purpose is not social entertainment; it is finding someone that you can team up with to make the world a better place as servants of God. This is the courtship procedure:

1. Boy and Girl establish themselves professionally, financially, emotionally and spiritually
2. Boy and Girl meet each other
3. Boy or Girl, together with their parents, decides that the other would be a good match for marriage and requests courtship
4. Courtship is set up and Boy and Girl get to know each other on an intellectual, spiritual and personal level
5. Boy and Girl decide that they are compatible for marriage
6. Boy and Girl get married and change the world together

Based on the principles of Heaven, this procedure ensures that men and women make wise choices for a life-partner; it allows decisions to be made based on actual characteristics and not purely on romance, feelings and the rush of hormones. As you go through this book you will understand this procedure a lot better. But more important than the procedure, you will understand the principles upon which the procedure is based.

Each courtship, each relationship, each love story is different. But the principles of God's Kingdom are unchanging. In your situation, you might not follow the exact steps written above and in this book. However, the principles on which the procedure is built are of vital importance. The procedure itself does not come from God. But the principles do. Whatever your situation or your unique relationship experience, may the Holy Spirit lead you to follow and to keep to the path of principle. You will find in most cases that the procedure makes following God's principles simple.

In this form the procedure follows the ideal scenario. In the book you will also find out what happens in not-so-ideal situations. Also, if you have not followed this procedure, and you have perhaps been hurt by the dating procedure, or you have hurt someone else by following the dating procedure, I hope you will decide to say "Goodbye" to the dating procedure and instead go with God's courtship principles.

Life's 3 important questions
Your single years are a great opportunity for building life-long friendships with people of the same sex and of the opposite sex. Never in your life will you have as much freedom to be able to build life-long friendships as when you are single. This is also the best time in your life to ask yourself and to make decisions on life's three most important questions:

1. What will I do with Jesus?
2. What will my life-work be?
3. Who will I marry?

I have placed these in order of their highest priority. By the time you get to question 3, you should already have made decisions on questions 1 and 2. Although this book is about courtship there is one subject that is more important than courtship or any other subject: your salvation.

> Seek ye first the kingdom of God and His righteousness.
>
> Matthew 6:33

The choice to follow Jesus is the most important decision. If you have not yet decided to follow Jesus all the way, then I invite you to do so before you continue reading this book. This book will focus mainly on questions 2 and 3, so it is important that you know where you stand with Jesus.

Each chapter in this book will discuss various aspects of the courtship procedure and the principles behind the steps. The first step in the courtship procedure is about finding joy and fulfilment in your life-work as a single person and to achieve excellence in that work. It is about doing and being all that God wants you to, based on the skills, talents, influence and opportunities that He has blessed you with. It is the most important step in the courtship procedure. If you skip this step, you may never find joy and fulfilment as a married person. Chapter 1 centres on this first step.

In Chapter 2 we focus on looking for a life-partner. We take a look at the purpose of marriage, what exactly to look for in a potential life-partner, and how to go about the search. In Chapter 3 we look at why it is important to get parents involved right from the start and we look specifically on the role of a girl's father in her life. Chapter 4 focuses on some of the specifics of courtship. It looks at what should and should not be done. In the last chapter we look at engagement and the wedding.

Enjoy this learning experience, discuss everything that you learn with your parents, your friends, family and most importantly speak to God about what you learn. I hope that your relationship experiences may be filled with joy, fulfilment and happiness as you apply the principles in this book.

Chapter One

Discovering Your Purpose

"As for these four youths, God gave them knowledge and skill in all learning and wisdom: and Daniel had understanding in all visions and dreams."

Daniel 1:17 (ESV)

Discovering Your Purpose

The most important step in the courtship procedure is the first step of establishing yourself professionally, financially, emotionally and spiritually. Discovering your purpose is a vital step in establishing yourself in these areas. A question you should ask yourself is: Where does God want me to work? God has a special place for you to work:

> Not more surely is the place prepared for us in the heavenly mansions than is the special place designated on earth where we are to work for God.
>
> *Christ's Object Lessons* pgs. 326, 327

If you enter into a courtship relationship with someone before discovering your purpose, you place yourself on dangerous grounds. One reason for this is that you may never discover your purpose because you will be bound by the needs of someone else. When you are in a relationship with someone, it becomes more difficult for you to find out what God wants of you because you are at the same time focussing on what your partner wants from you. This is why Paul writes:

> An unmarried man can spend his time doing the Lord's work and thinking how to please him. But a married man can't do that so well. He has to think about his earthly responsibilities and how to please his wife.
>
> 1 Corinthians 7:32 (NLT)

Paul goes on to say that it is the same with a single woman. Whenever you enter into a relationship with someone, especially a deeply emotional relationship like courtship, your decisions will be affected by the person that you are in a relationship with. You are at a time in your life when you are deciding on what your life-work will be, and it is important that you make that decision purely on what God wants and not what anyone else wants.

When I was in primary school, grade 5, all the pupils in the grade went on a trip to a small town in Mpumalanga called Waterval Boven. The name of the town means "above the waterfall" because there is a beautiful waterfall in that town. It is near impossible to manage 150 students all in one go, so we were divided into 2 groups. The first group would leave for Waterval

The time and freedom that you have as a single person is the perfect set of circumstances to discover your purpose.

Boven on Monday and come back on Wednesday. The second group was to leave on Wednesday and come back on Friday. We were allowed to choose which group we wanted to be in. All we had to do was to write our names on the corresponding list in classroom window of one of our teachers, Mrs Bailey.

In grade 5, there was a pretty girl that I was interested in. Jamie-Lee (I have used pseudonyms throughout the book). She had long black hair, and fair, soft skin. She had the sweetest voice and wonderful personality. I went to Mrs Bailey's classroom and I looked to see where Jamie-Lee and her friends had written their names. They were going with the first group. During break time that day I persuaded my friends that we should go with the first group. And we did.

A silly example, but it demonstrates how small and sometimes big decisions can be influenced by the person that we are most attracted to. Imagine then how much more influence a courting relationship will have on your decisions. The time and freedom that you have as a single person is the perfect set of circumstances to discover your purpose. You do not have to make that decision based on any responsibilities other than your responsibility to God. Now is the time to find out where God wants you to work. We will talk about how a little later on. Discovering your purpose first will allow you to link up with someone who will complement that purpose, and you will both go on to do and to achieve greater things for God.

Very often as young people, instead of focussing on what God wants, we find someone we like and make some decisions so that we can be with that person. And then we go with that. And maybe it doesn't work out, so we end that relationship and make some decisions to be with the next person that we are interested in. At the end of the day, we never really find out what God wants. Or, we find out too late. This is why there is so much mediocrity in the church today. This is why we find couples that are just "average" instead of being the spectacular change-makers in the world and in the church that God wants them to be.

This brings me to the second reason why discovering your purpose is the first step. Suppose you do get into a relationship with someone before discovering your purpose. And suppose you marry this person. Suppose then after you get married you manage to discover your purpose. Now, you may be unable to fulfil your purpose because of the responsibility that you have towards the person you are married to. I know of one person who, only after getting married, realized that God wants him to study theology and to become a pastor. But, because of his wife's desires, and his responsibility towards his children, he was not able to go. You may also find yourself on the opposite end; you may be the one that is making it impossible for your life-partner to fulfil their purpose in life.

As an extreme example, suppose God wants you to be in China. Yet, He wants the person that you are courting to be in Brazil. But, the two of you are so head-over-heels for each other that by the time you are married, you find yourselves in West Africa. The Kingdom of God suffers and the good that you may have done for millions of people does not happen simply because you did not find out what God wanted of you before getting into a relationship.

God set an example for us when He created Adam:

> The Lord God placed the man in the Garden of Eden to tend and care for it.
> Genesis 2:15 (NLT)

God first gave Adam work before He gave him a wife, even before He let him see her.

Glorifying God
We love God. As we walk with Him daily, and as we spend time each day in personal devotion our love for Him grows stronger. One of our purposes as created beings is to glorify God. Because of our love for God, we are motivated and fuelled to fulfil this purpose of glorifying Him in everything that we do. Isaiah 43:7 tells us that God created us for His glory. God is glorified when we develop and use our talents according to His will.

> It is the purpose of God to glorify Himself in His people before the world. He expects those who bear the name of Christ to represent Him in thought, word, and deed. Their thoughts are to be pure and their words noble and

uplifting, drawing those around them nearer the Saviour. The religion of Christ is to be interwoven with all that they do and say. Their every business transaction is to be fragrant with the presence of God.

Christian Service pg. 26

Notice that Ellen White says "every business transaction". Glorifying God does not necessarily mean that you are going to be a missionary, a colporteur, a pastor or an evangelist. These are callings. And you should never do any of these unless you are sure that God has called you to them. But it is not necessary to follow in these lines of work in order to bring glory to God. Humans will bring glory to God's name throughout eternity, yet, in heaven, you can be sure that there will be no missionaries, colporteurs, pastors or evangelists. So, how then will we glorify God in heaven? In the same way we are to glorify Him now: by using and improving the talents that He has given us we glorify God.

All right inventions and improvements have their source in Him who is wonderful in counsel and excellent in working. The skilful touch of the physician's hand, his power over nerve and muscle, his knowledge of the delicate organism of the body, is the wisdom of divine power, to be used in behalf of the suffering. The skill with which the carpenter uses the hammer, the strength with which the blacksmith makes the anvil ring, comes from God. He has entrusted men with talents, and He expects them to look to Him for counsel. Whatever we do, in whatever department of the work we are placed, He desires to control our minds that we may do perfect work. Religion and business are not two separate things; they are one. Bible religion is to be interwoven with all we do or say. Divine and human agencies are to combine in temporal as well as in spiritual achievements. They are to be united in all human pursuits, in mechanical and agricultural labors, in mercantile and scientific enterprises. There must be co-operation in everything embraced in Christian activity.

Christ's Object Lessons pg. 349

Pastors, colporteurs and evangelists are not the only people who can share their faith and study the Bible with people. We can build relationships with those around us, gain their trust and then share our faith with them.

The religion of the Bible is not to be confined between the covers of a book, nor within the walls of a church. It is not to be brought out occasionally for our own benefit, and then to be carefully laid aside again. It is to sanctify the daily life, to manifest itself in every business transaction and in all our social relations.

Christian Service pg. 26

God has given each one of us skills that we should improve by studying and training so that we can perform our life-work to the best of our ability. And wherever we work, we will meet people with whom we can build relationships. This may be the only place these people ever come into contact with the Advent message.

God desires that we should make a success of our lives by making use of and cultivating the talents that He has blessed us with. To use and develop these talents is to be human; it is a vital part of our design. To neglect the development of our talents is deny our own humanity. You need this continual upward trail and pursuit in order to be complete as a human being. Aim for greatness, aim for success, aim for continual development. This attitude will keep you from sinking into despair, despondency, and discouragement.

The mind and heart need culture daily, and neglect will be productive of evil. The more natural ability God has bestowed upon an individual, the greater the improvement he is required to make, and the greater his responsibility to use his time and talents for the glory of God. The mind must not remain dormant. If it is not exercised in the acquisition of knowledge, there will be a sinking into ignorance, superstition, and fancy. If the intellectual faculties are not cultivated as they should be to glorify God, they will become strong and powerful aids in leading to perdition.

Testimonies for the Church vol. 4 pg. 442

The principle of being excellent in our life-work is found in many places in the Bible. Paul says in his letter to the Romans that we should be

Not slothful in business.

Romans 12:11

And Solomon says in the book of wisdom

Seest thou a man diligent in his business? he shall stand before kings; he shall not stand before mean men.

Proverbs 22:29

In performing our work to the best of our ability and by cultivating excellence therein, God is glorified. He wishes above all things that we should prosper. And when we prosper by the correct application and cultivation of our talents, He is glorified.

Education is about improving your talents; it is about becoming useful to humanity.

The Economy

Have you ever asked yourself what the economy is? Everyday millions of business transactions take place in the world. People everywhere are trading money for products and services. The economy is a system in which men and women work to add value and to improve the lives of others. Any business that does not add value to the life of another person does not last. The business goes bankrupt.

> The student must be impressed that he has it in his power, by combining grace with effort, to make himself a man. The mental and physical capabilities with which God has adorned him may by cultivation and painstaking effort become a power to benefit his fellow men.
>
> *Evangelism* pg. 668

You may have wondered why you have to go to school to get an education. You may have wondered why you have to go to university. Education is not about making a lot of money. Education is about improving your talents; it is about becoming useful to humanity. If you are not educated, you become a burden to humanity. When you are educated, you become useful to humanity.

Have you ever considered the work that butterflies do for us? Butterflies are pollinators. As they go from flower to flower to collect nectar, they cause the male parts of the flowers to come into contact with the female parts. This causes fruit to develop. A lot of the fruit that we have depends on these little creatures going from flower to flower to pollinate the flowers.

If they didn't do their work, there are some fruits that we would not have. Their work is pollination. The nectar is a reward, or a payment, for the work that they do.

In the same way, each of us has a work to do to benefit other people. It may be as a nurse, a receptionist, a teacher, a builder, a truck driver, an engineer, or an accountant. Whatever the work may be, we must remember that we are doing it to help our fellow human beings. When we get paid for it, it is like the nectar that a butterfly receives for pollinating flowers.

In the Jewish economy that we read about in the Bible, each person had a trade, or a skill that they used to provide a service to someone else. It was the responsibility of a Jewish father to teach his son a trade. And it was the responsibility of a Jewish mother to teach her daughter about homemaking and the duties involved in homemaking. Why did each person need a trade? Because there were needs in the community that were to be met. Jesus was a carpenter. He was taught to be a carpenter by His father, Joseph. Why? Because people needed chairs and cabinets and all those things that carpenters make that people need. Ellen White says of Jesus,

> He was doing God's service just as much when labouring at the carpenter's bench as when working miracles for the multitude.
>
> *Desire of Ages* pg. 74

It is also interesting to note that of the twelve tribes of Israel, only one tribe was called to do full-time ministerial work—the Levites. Every other tribe had a different part to play in the Jewish economy. As important as the work of gospel ministry is, God has not called every one of us to full-time ministry. I am speaking here of being a pastor, evangelist, or colporteur on a full-time basis. God has designed also that some of us become doctors, others engineers, writers, teachers, physicists and so on, with the intention that we will develop the skills that He has given us and that we benefit other people.

> The Lord desires to have in His service intelligent men, men qualified for various lines of work. There is need of business men who will weave the grand principles of truth into all their transactions. And their talents should be perfected by most thorough study and training. If men in any line of

work need to improve their opportunities to become wise and efficient, it is those who are using their ability in building up the kingdom of God in our world. Of Daniel we learn that in all his business transactions, when subjected to the closest scrutiny, not one fault or error could be found. He was a sample of what every business man may be. His history shows what may be accomplished by one who consecrates the strength of brain and bone and muscle, of heart and life, to the service of God.

Messages to Young People pg. 222

God has placed men in the world, and it is their privilege to eat, to drink, to trade, to marry, and to be given in marriage; but it is safe to do these things only in the fear of God.

Messages to Young People pg. 456

Don't think that because you are not doing full-time gospel ministry work that you are not fulfilling God's will for your life. He has put us on earth and it is our privilege to have enjoyment in things that He has given us, to trade, or to do business, and to get married. As long as we are enjoying these privileges while keeping the principles that God has given us in His word, then we are in His will.

What are your ambitions in life? Is it to be popular amongst the guys, or the girls? Or do you desire to make a difference in the lives of others. Do you just want to have fun, and spend your precious time on the many meaningless amusements that are available for youth today? Or do you desire to use your time to improve and make use of the talents, skills and opportunities that God has blessed you with. Do you just want to make a lot of money so that you can travel the world on a cruise ship? God has created you for greater things than that.

Teach [the youth] that life's true aim is not to secure the greatest possible gain for themselves, but to honor their Maker in doing their part of the world's work, and lending a helpful hand to those weaker or more ignorant.

Education pg. 221

Here is one of my favourite statements in all of Spirit of Prophecy:

Dear youth, what is the aim and purpose of your life? Are you ambitious for education that you may have a name and position in the world? Have you thoughts that you dare not express, that you may one day stand upon the summit of intellectual greatness; that you may sit in deliberative and legislative councils, and help to enact laws for the nation? There is nothing wrong in these aspirations. You may every one of you make your mark. You should be content with no mean attainments. Aim high, and spare no pains to reach the standard.

Messages to Young People pg. 36

Heavenly Occupation

When you think about the activities that will keep us busy in heaven, what comes to your mind? For many people, when thinking about activities in heaven, they think about just sitting on a cloud all day and playing the harp, or something similar. God has created us with much more skill and ability than what is needed to play a harp. Now, I'll admit, it does take quite a bit of skill to play a harp, but you can be sure that playing the harp is not all that we will be doing.

We cannot suppose that when the final triumph shall come, and we have the mansions prepared for us, idleness will be our portion—that we shall rest in a blissful, do-nothing state. In the earth made new, the redeemed will engage in the occupations and pleasures that brought happiness to Adam and Eve in the beginning. The Eden life will be lived, the life in garden and field. "They shall build houses, and inhabit them; and they shall plant vineyards, and eat the fruit of them. They shall not build, and another inhabit; they shall not plant, and another eat: for as the days of a tree are the days of my people, and mine elect shall long enjoy the work of their hands." Isaiah 65:21, 22.

There I saw most glorious houses, that had the appearance of silver, supported by four pillars set with pearls most glorious to behold. These were to be inhabited by the saints. In each was a golden shelf. I saw many of the saints go into the houses, take off their glittering crowns and lay them on the shelf, then go out into the field by the houses to do something with the earth; not as we have to do with the earth here; no, no. A glorious light shone all about their heads, and they were continually shouting and offering praises to God.

Every faculty will be developed, every capacity increased. The acquirement of knowledge will not weary the mind or exhaust the energies. There the grandest enterprises may be carried forward, the loftiest aspirations reached, the highest ambitions realized; and still there will arise new heights to surmount, new wonders to admire, new truths to comprehend, fresh objects to call forth the powers of mind and soul and body.

There will be work to do in heaven. Just like we have occupations here on earth to benefit each other, we will have occupations in heaven to benefit each other. We will use our brains and our muscles as we serve each other and as we serve God. Before Adam and Eve sinned they had work to do in the Garden of Eden. After they sinned, they still had work to do, but the ground was cursed and it became very difficult to get good results from doing work. It is in God's design that we work, but in heaven our work will not be contaminated with evil as it is now.

Have you ever wondered if there will be mathematics and physics in heaven? Well, think for a moment what mathematics and physics are. Mathematics and physics are both the study of nature and the patterns found in nature. Blaise Pascal, Leonard Euler, Gauss, Newton and many of the early scientists looked at nature and realized that the universe was intelligently designed, and that it operated according to fixed laws. And they made it their life-work to study these laws.

Realizing also that there was one Designer that designed and created all things, many of them became inventors of useful devices that they knew would work because of the laws that were set in place by the Creator. Aeroplanes, cars, computers and electricity all work because scientists have applied the laws of God in nature to build devices that improve our lives. The natural laws work in all aspects of life because there is one Designer. Therefore, we can use these laws to build devices that we can use to benefit each other.

Science, biology and geography are all studies of the creation of God. The theorems and laws that the mathematicians and physicists have written down are the laws that God has set in place when He designed the universe. Newton's laws of motion are really God's laws described in a language that we can understand. So, will there be mathematics in heaven? Well, maybe we will not call it mathematics, but we will forever be studying the things that God has created. However, as Ellen White writes, it will not make us tired; it will not hurt our brains or stress us out. We will enjoy every moment of it.

What other occupations will there be in heaven? Isaiah says that we will build houses. So perhaps there will be a lot of designing, building, architecture, perhaps engineering. A lot of space travel, I'm sure. Certainly no doctors, though we do need doctors now. But we will not be doing nothing. We will be developing our skills and talents and using them to benefit each other. And we can start living like that while here on earth. Getting an education is not just about this life. Getting an education, developing your skills and talents, studying to gain knowledge and understanding of the universe is something that will continue in heaven and throughout eternity. Now is the time to start.

Blessed is that servant

Sometimes when we think about heaven and about the end of the world and the second coming of Jesus, it makes us lose our ambition to do great things while here on earth. You may think to yourself, "Why get a good education, Jesus is coming", or "Why study hard for my test, why get a distinction, this world is not my home". Do you ever feel like that? Do you ever feel that it does not make sense to be brilliant at the things of this world because we are destined for heaven? Or do you maybe feel that every line of work except the gospel ministry is meaningless? Let's look again at what Ellen White says about Jesus:

> He was doing God's service just as much when labouring at the carpenter's bench as when working miracles for the multitude. And every youth who follows Christ's example of faithfulness and obedience in His lowly home may claim those words spoken of Him by the Father through the Holy Spirit, "Behold My Servant, whom I uphold; Mine Elect, in whom My soul delighteth." Isaiah 42:1
>
> *Desire of Ages* pg. 74

Jesus did not think to Himself that the work He was doing as a carpenter was meaningless. For Him, He was working for God while making chairs and cupboards. When we are faithful in doing the work that we have been given, we are doing God's work faithfully. When we are improving our skills and talents, we are doing God's work.

God has put us in charge of the skills, talents and opportunities that He has given us. Jesus said the following about a servant who was put in charge of some things by his master:

Blessed is that servant, whom his lord when he cometh shall find so doing.

Matthew 24:46

In other words, when the master comes back from his journey and he finds that the servant is doing what he was supposed to be doing, that servant is a blessed servant. What is the job that Jesus, our Master, has given us? That we glorify Him with what He has given us. Just like the servant in the story, the work that God has given us to do is an ongoing work; it doesn't stop even when we go to heaven. So, He expects us always to be improving what He has given us. We will continue to improve and grow even in heaven.

When I was younger my parents used to give my sisters and me certain chores to do at home. We were to do these chores when we got home from school and they were to be done before our parents got home from work. It may have been cooking, cleaning or working in the yard. Very often I was lazy and didn't do what I was required. I would spend the afternoon playing with the neighbours, watching television or playing computer games. However, I would get a really warm feeling inside if my parents got home and I was busy doing what they had asked me to do.

If Jesus comes back to earth tomorrow, and He finds that we are glorifying His name by making use of our skills and talents, He will say:

"Well done, thou good and faithful servant: thou hast been faithful over a few things, I will make thee ruler over many things: enter thou into the joy of thy lord."

Matthew 25:21

It doesn't matter what work we are doing, whether it is school work, church work, office work, house work, yard work. As long as we are doing work that honours Him, He will say to us "Well done, thou good and faithful servant."

When Jesus comes, He will find you busy. But what will you busy with? If He comes and He finds that you were just waiting around for His coming, doing nothing with the gifts that He has given you, you will be like the unfaithful servant to whom the master says "Take the talent from him, and give it unto him which had ten talents." But if He comes and He says to you, "What were you doing?" and you say "I was studying to become a doctor (or builder, or engineer), improving the intellect that you gave me so that I can be a servant to other people", He will say "Well done, thou good and faithful servant."

When our Lord returns, He will find us busy doing something. The question is, "Busy doing what?"

If Jesus comes and He asks "What were you doing with your money?" and you say "Some I gave for offering, and some I was saving up so that I could buy property so that I can look after a family one day." Jesus will say "Well done, thou good and faithful servant: you have been faithful over few things, I will make you ruler over many things." I think you get the idea. The fact that Jesus is coming soon does not mean that we should sit around and do nothing but wait. It actually makes it more urgent for us to get busy doing something with what He has blessed us with because "blessed is that servant, whom his lord when he cometh shall find so doing."

When our Lord returns, He will find us busy doing something. The question is, "Busy doing what?" Will we be glorifying His name by attempting some great work, improving the talents that He has given us, doing a work to benefit humanity? Or sitting around, waiting? Get busy doing something.

Am I ready for marriage?
The first question to ask yourself is "Am I perfectly happy to stay single for as long as this is God's will for my life?" If you cannot give a definite "Yes!" then you are most-likely not yet ready for marriage; you are not content to be single, therefore you will not be content as a married person. And if you are not yet ready for marriage, you are not yet ready to be in a one-on-one relationship with someone of the opposite sex.

Maybe you have not yet discovered where God wants you to work. Give it some time. Stay single until you have sorted this out between you and God. Being single gives you the opportunity to try things and go places without any restrictions. For as long as you are single, you have the option of getting married. But once you are married, you don't have the option of being single. Sort out your life-work decisions and achievements before you even think about courting. Become content being single, and only then give courting a chance.

There are three things that you must have before you even consider courtship. The first is an education. The second is a job, or a way of earning an income. For the third, take a look at the following statement from Spirit of Prophecy:

> Many have entered the marriage relation who have not acquired property, and who have had no inheritance. They did not possess physical strength or mental energy to acquire property. It has been just such ones who have been in haste to marry, and who have taken upon themselves responsibilities of which they had no just sense. They did not possess noble, elevated feelings, and had no just idea of the duty of a husband and father, and what it would cost them to provide for the wants of a family. And they manifested no more propriety in the increase of their families than that shown in their business transactions.
>
> *Messages to Young People* pg. 461

The third requirement is property. Property refers to land, money, a car or other resources that can be used to provide for the needs of a family. But the statement above speaks about marriage, right? How does it apply to where you are? Well, let's say you start courting someone tomorrow. On average, courtship will last for two years and then a couple might decide to get married. So, in two years from now, will you and your partner have acquired enough property to support the needs of each other as an independent married couple? Or, will you have enough money saved up, or have built up other assets, to be able to provide for the needs of a family? If not, then you are not ready for courtship and it would be wise for you to pause the relationship until you have worked at your life-work long and hard enough for you to be able to do so. This is especially so if you are a young man, because it is your responsibility as a man to make sure that your family has everything that it needs.

You may say, "Well, we are not taking things serious yet." This is where the difference between dating and courting becomes clearer. Why are you together then if you are not serious yet? There is not a single example in the Bible of people who were together just because they liked each other. Or because they wanted to hang out. Or kiss now and then. Courtship is about marriage. A one-on-one relationship with someone of the opposite

ABOUT COURTSHIP

31

sex that is not a means of determining whether or not the person will be a good marriage partner is an invention of Satan. It also makes you unavailable to someone who may be serious.

If you desire to be with someone without the intention of getting married, you are playing Satan's game of dating. The result of playing this game is emotional, spiritual and sometimes physical ruin. This is not God's plan for your life. God wants you always to consider marriage whenever you enter into a relationship with someone. And if you are not yet ready for marriage, then it is not God's will for you to be in a relationship with someone.

Satan's plan is to keep you from enjoying the benefits of being single: finding God's purpose for your life and becoming ready financially, spiritually and emotionally to be married. The way he does this is by getting you into a relationship with someone who also does not yet know God's purpose for their life and is also not yet ready for marriage. This keeps you both from finding God's purpose for your lives and from becoming mature and spiritually strong heads of a family.

High school is not the time to be entering into a courting relationship:

> While at school, students should not allow their minds to become confused by thoughts of courtship. They are there to gain a fitness to work for God, and this thought is ever to be uppermost.
>
> *Counsels to Parents, Teachers and Students* pg. 100

College, university or trade-school is not the time to be entering into a relationship. Finish the basic training for your life-work first before entering into a relationship. The following statement was made about Battle Creek College, a tertiary school:

> Some of those who attend the college do not properly improve their time. Full of the buoyancy of youth, they spurn the restraint that is brought to bear upon them. Especially do they rebel against the rules that will not allow young gentlemen to pay their attentions to young ladies. Full well is known the evil of such a course in this degenerate age. In a college where so many youth are associated, imitating the customs of the world in this respect would turn the thoughts in a channel that would hinder them in their pursuit of knowledge and in their interest in religious things.

The infatuation on the part of both young men and women in thus placing the affections upon each other during school days shows a lack of good judgment. … Under this bewitching delusion the momentous responsibility felt by every sincere Christian is laid aside, spirituality dies, and the judgment and eternity lose their awful significance.

Every faculty of those who become affected by this contagious disease—blind love—is brought in subjection to it. They seem to be devoid of good sense, and their course of action is disgusting to all who behold it. … With many the crisis of the disease is reached in an immature marriage, and when the novelty is past and the bewitching power of love-making is over, one or both parties awake to their true situation. They then find themselves ill-mated, but united for life.

Testimonies for the Church vol. 5 pg. 110

Until you are prepared for your life-work, you are not yet ready for marriage. There should be two things on your mind: gaining knowledge and growing spiritually. This is the statement that made me realize that it was not God's will for my life, or any other young person's life, to be in a relationship while still preparing for life-work.

A young Christian man who is serious about becoming the best husband he can be will not waste any time on relationships while he is still in high school or studying and training to perform his life-work. He will focus on the main task: getting ready for his life-work. He will finish high school on time, with marks good enough to get into the university, college, or trade-school he needs to go to. He will finish university, college or trade-school on time. He will get a job or start a business, and he will save up enough money or other property to be able to provide for his family.

A young Christian woman who is serious about becoming the best wife she can be will also not waste any time on a relationship while she is still in high school or studying and training to perform her life-work. She will not be entertained by young men who have not finished high school and trained for their life-work. She will not consider becoming involved with a young man who is not financially stable.

Another question you can ask yourself is "Am I faithful in my duties at home?"

It is by faithfulness to duty in the parental home that the youth are to prepare themselves for homes of their own. Let them here practice self-denial, and manifest kindness, courtesy, and Christian sympathy. Thus love will be kept warm in the heart, and he who goes out from such a household to stand at the head of a family of his own will know how to promote the happiness of her whom he has chosen as a companion for life. Marriage, instead of being the end of love, will be only its beginning.

Messages to Young People pg. 466

Young man, can you fix things? Young woman, can you cook? True love is not about romance or feeling warm inside. True love is when two people who understand what it takes to run a family and a household come together and take care of each other's needs. Home is the place where you learn how to love your future husband or wife. If you are faithful in your home duties, you will make a good husband or wife.

Since both men and women have a part in home-making, boys as well as girls should gain a knowledge of household duties. To make a bed and put a room in order, to wash dishes, to prepare a meal, to wash and repair his own clothing, is a training that need not make any boy less manly; it will make him happier and more useful. And if girls, in turn, could learn to harness and drive a horse, and to use the saw and the hammer, as well as the rake and the hoe, they would be better fitted to meet the emergencies of life.

Education pg. 216

If you are in a relationship with someone right now and you have not yet completed high school, college, university or trade school, I urge you to discuss what you are reading in this chapter with that person, and think critically about where you are versus where God wants you to be. Are you spending time on a relationship that could rather be spent on improving your marks at school, or increasing your Bible knowledge, or in growing closer to God? It is not God's will for your life to be in a relationship during this critical period of your life.

I decided that it would be best to end the relationship. I had briefly started dating a young lady from church when I came across this light. Erin and I had only been on one date, so the relationship wasn't very deep yet. She was still in high school, and I was at the end of my second year at university.

When I discovered what I have shared with you in this chapter, I called Erin and told her that we needed to talk. I went to her house and I shared with her what I had found. I really didn't want to hurt her feelings. I didn't want her to think that I was not going to go on another date with her because there was something wrong with her. I wanted her to know that it was because I had come to realize that it was not God's plan for our lives for us to be in a relationship. My words were something like this: "I like you. But, we are both still young and not ready for relationships according to God's standard."

I don't know if Erin made the same decision to stay single until she had completed school. I hope she did. As I mentioned before, making that decision was one of the best things I have ever done for my spiritual, mental and professional development. This is what I hoped for her as well. This is what I hope for every young person. Get out while the relationship is still young. The longer you stay in it, the harder it will be to end it if you find out that it does not fit in with the work that God wants you to do.

> Your happiness in life is not determined by your circumstances in life, but by your attitude to life.

Single and Gifted
Your happiness in life is not determined by your circumstances in life, but by your attitude to life. Being single can be hard. Very hard. But being married can also be hard. Life can be hard. To enjoy being single, it is not your circumstances that need to change, and you don't have to convince yourself that being single is amazing. You just need to change your attitude to your situation. You can do this by being thankful for the blessings that God has given you as a single person. You can do this by praising and thanking God for giving you everything that you need today for your day to be meaningful.

> In every thing give thanks: for this is the will of God in Christ Jesus concerning you.
>
> 1 Thessalonians 5:18

Singleness is a gift. And you are a gifted person. Feelings of loneliness may come when you are single. And they may be very strong. But these feelings come and go. Feelings tell you that it will be pleasurable to get into a relationship. But they don't tell you when and with whom to get into a relationship. You need the powers of reasoning and judgement to make those decisions. Acknowledge that the feelings are there, but allow your higher powers of reasoning, conscience and judgement to help you to decide whether or not you should get married. Do not make the decision based on your feelings alone.

Singleness is a time to discover yourself and to discover yourself in God. Singleness is a time to see whether or not you will follow God while there is no one in your life making it difficult for you to do what you think is best. Singleness is a time to see whether or not you will be on time for church when there is no one influencing your decision. Singleness is a time to go where God wants you to go, to be what He wants you to be, and to do what He wants you to do without having to consider the needs of someone else.

Singleness is a time to learn a new language, or two. A time to travel the world. A time to be a missionary in a foreign country. Singleness is the time to become a business person, an entrepreneur, and to create jobs for other people. Singleness is a time to learn to play an instrument. The world has a lot to offer a single person—things that God has given us the privilege to enjoy with thanksgiving. Conquer the feelings of loneliness and you have access to these joys. Allow the feelings to conquer you and you may find yourself married, in your mid-40's, and thinking to yourself "Where did all the time go?" The book of wisdom tells us:

> Give not thy strength unto women, nor thy ways to that which destroyeth kings.
>
> Proverbs 31:3

Satan's plan is to keep you in a relationship so that you do not become the king or queen that God has given you the potential to become. So he gets you involved with one person, and then another, and then another. Getting you to move from one relationship to the next, spending the strength and vigour of your youth on relationships and never getting to enjoy the benefits of singleness. Young man, do not give your strength to women. Young lady, do not give your strength to men. Don't spend the best years of your life trying to make relationships work. Enjoy the gifts that God has given you as a single person. The time for marriage will come, if God wills it.

In the next chapter we will look at another step in the courtship procedure: looking for someone to court. What things should you look for in a life mate? How involved should your parents be? These questions will be answered in the next chapter. You will not be ready for the next step until you have discovered your purpose, finished school and trained for your life-work. But even if you haven't yet completed this step, read on, it may come in handy one day when you have completed it.

Summary

Discover your purpose. Take a look at your life and think about the skills, talents and opportunities that God has given you. Ask Him for guidance as you choose a life-work. He is the one who gave you your gifts, and if you ask Him, He will help you to make a decision that will bring you fulfilment in life and will glorify His name. Be faithful in your school work and in your house work. Whatever you choose for a life-work, get proper training and education for this work so that you will be able to do it to the best of your ability. Make the most of your single days; enjoy the gifts and freedom that come with it. Thank God each day for the blessings He has given you.

Chapter Two

Looking for a Partner

"Whoso findeth a wife findeth a good thing, and obtaineth favour of the Lord."

Proverbs 18:22

Looking for a Partner

So, you've discovered your purpose, you have finished school, you have trained for your life-work, and you have a job, or a business. You are now ready for marriage. Yay! What now? Well, do you want to get married? Why? This chapter will look at some of the reasons why you may want to get married as well as God's purpose for marriage. If you understand God's purpose for marriage it will help you to understand why it is important to make a good choice for a life-partner. The chapter also looks at some of the important things to look for when looking for a marriage partner and also how to go about the search.

Why get married?

To answer this question, let's go to the story of creation and take a look at why God created marriage:

> And the Lord God said, It is not good that man should be alone; I will make him an help meet for him.
>
> Genesis 2:18

God said that it is not good that man should be alone. Ellen White writes about this verse:

> Man was not made to dwell in solitude; he was to be a social being. Without companionship the beautiful scenes and delightful employments of Eden would have failed to yield perfect happiness. Even communion with angels could not have satisfied his desire for sympathy and companionship. There was none of the same nature to love and to be loved.
>
> Patriarchs and Prophets pg. 46

God has blessed us with the privilege of marriage so that we may have someone to enjoy the good things of life. Remember that Adam was the only human being on earth at the time, so he didn't even have friends. In our day there are billions of human beings on the planet, so we do not experience loneliness the way that Adam felt it. We have the companionship of friends, parents, cousins, schoolmates, fellow church members, and then of course there is the special companionship of a marriage partner.

God created us to be social beings. Genesis 1:27 tells us that God created us in His image. God is also a social being. In the Godhead there is relationship. When God made Adam and Adam was alone, humanity was not yet a complete reflection of God, because there was no relationship. How could Adam love if there was no one to love? How could Adam share if there was no one to share with? Adam could only fully express God's character if there was someone with him to benefit from him expressing God's character.

When you are single, very often you live life for yourself and you only care about your own needs and wants. This is selfish behaviour. Being married teaches you to care for the needs of someone else; it teaches you to be considerate; it teaches you self-denial; it teaches you where you have defects in your character.

> Those who marry enter a school from which they are never in this life to be graduated.
>
> *The Adventist Home* pg. 105

> Iron sharpeneth iron; so a man sharpeneth the countenance of his friend.
>
> Proverbs 27:17

Marriage is a school like no other.

No other person in the whole world will know you as well as the person that you marry. No other person in the world will love you and desire good for you as much as the person you marry. There will be no better person who can help you to get rid of your bad character traits than the person whom you marry. Another reason, then, to get married, is for character development. Marriage is a school like no other.

Solomon writes:

> Two are better than one; because they have a good reward for their labour. For if they fall, the one will lift up his fellow: but woe to him that is alone when he falleth; for he hath not another to help him up.
>
> Ecclesiastes 4:9-10

In this verse, Solomon repeats the companionship reason for marriage:

someone to share your joys, sorrows, achievements and disappointments with. But he also gives us another reason: balancing your strengths and weaknesses. You may be weak in one area, but if the person you are married to is strong in this area, they can help you. Note also, that Solomon suggests that you can fall. If you do fall, and you do have a need, it is important that the person you are married to is spiritually strong in this area to be able to help you back up.

Solomon gives us another reason to get married:

> Drink water from your own cistern, and running water from your own well. . . . And rejoice with the wife of your youth. As a loving deer and a graceful doe, Let her breasts satisfy you at all times; and always be enraptured with her love.
>
> Proverbs 5:15, 18-19

God has given us sexual desire, and getting married allows us to enjoy the gift of sex. If it were not for sexual desire, some people would never get married nor have children. God has also given us the privilege of having sex. The senses that God has given us allow us to enjoy the good things that He has given us here on earth. Our taste-buds allow us to enjoy delicious food. Our ears allow us to enjoy beautiful music. Our eyes allow us to enjoy the wonderful sights to be seen in nature. Even so, our sexual organs allow us to enjoy God's gift of sex.

Sexual desire may drive you to want to get married, but it is not a good enough guide to show you whom you should marry. Also, do not think that all your sexual desires will be fulfilled once you get married, or that you will never be sexually frustrated. You may sometimes be sexually frustrated as a single person. But it can be much more frustrating to be married and have your partner deny you sexually. It happens. Sometimes it's for a silly reason. And it can be worse than when you are single because when you are married you are seeing your spouse every morning or evening walking about in their underwear or naked.

Sexual desire must be kept under control. Getting married gives you the privilege of being sexually intimate with someone of the opposite sex, but it does not mean that you can fulfil all those sexual fantasies that you may have had throughout your life. God has given us senses to enjoy food, but he expects us not to over-eat. In the same way, He has given us sex for our enjoyment, but we must not have too much sex, nor sex that is displeasing to God. A woman who fears God will not only understand her husband's unique appetite for sex, but she will also not allow him to be intemperate. A man who fears God will always keep in mind that his wife's body is the temple of the Holy Spirit and not a mere machine created for his own pleasure.

Singleness is also a time to become strong in controlling your sexual desire. Marriage does not take away your temptation to have sex with someone that you are not married to. Marriage is not the solution to your sexual temptation. Marriage only allows you to enjoy the gift of sex that God has given to man. The solution to your sexual temptation is to abide in Christ, to get help from Him when you are tempted and to look to Him for strength and victory over sin. If you can do this as a single person, you will be more able to do it as a married person when you are tempted to commit adultery.

Marriage is a spiritual thing. A person who cannot make decisions based on the guidance of the Holy Spirit is not ready for marriage. A person who does not have a strong relationship with God will not make a good life-partner. A person who is not willing to change in character does not understand what marriage is about. Very often in marriage you will be required to do things that you do not want to but know you must do because of the needs of the person that you are married to. Only someone who is following Jesus and the guidance of His Spirit can minister to the needs of someone else even when not feeling like it.

"The One" vs. "A Good Match"
Does God have one special "soul mate" for you that you will find one day when He feels the time is right? Or has He given you the choice to decide when to get married and to decide whom to marry? The examples that we have in the Bible show us that both are possibilities. In Adam's case, there was only one person for him to marry; Eve was the one specially made for Adam to marry. The same is true in Isaac's case; God specially appointed Rebekah to be "the one" that Isaac was to marry. In Hosea's case, God told him to marry the prostitute, Gomer.

These were all special cases though. With Adam, it was the start of the world. With Isaac, there was not a group of ladies for him to choose from; Abraham sent his servant Eliezer to go find a wife for Isaac, and God showed Him whom He had appointed by a special sign. With Hosea, marrying Gomer was an object lesson to the Israelites to demonstrate God's love for His people. In general, however, God gives us the freedom to choose whom we will marry. Consider the following text:

> This is what the Lord commands concerning the daughters of Zelophehad: "Let them marry whom they think best, only they shall marry within the clan of the tribe of their father."
>
> Numbers 36:6 (ESV)

God's command to these ladies was that they marry whoever they thought best. So, they were required to do the thinking themselves, and to make a choice according to what they thought would be best. God also gave them boundaries; He said "Only marry within the clan of your father's tribe." It is the same with us; God has given us mental ability to be able to make well thought-out decisions, and He has also given us boundaries. God allows us to choose to marry whom we think best. But we must think things through.

Aside from Adam, Isaac and Hosea, you will struggle to find an example in the Bible where God says "Marry this specific person." God always gives us a choice in the matter, but He also gives us principles on which to base our choice. He says, for example, through Paul:

> Be ye not unequally yoked together with unbelievers.
>
> 2 Corinthians 6:14

The same is true in Spirit of Prophecy; you will struggle to find Ellen White counselling someone that "This is not the one that God has appointed for you" or "You should marry this particular person." Instead, she uses statements such as "This person is not a good match for you," or "Those who choose to marry." Even in the case of Isaac, Ellen White states:

In the mind of Abraham the choice of a wife for his son was a matter of grave importance; he was anxious to have him marry one who would not lead him from God.

Patriarchs and Prophets pg. 171

These statements show us that God has given the choice to us. However, He expects us to keep to the principles that He has given us when we make the choice.

It can be dangerous to believe that God has appointed one special person for you. It is also very easy to fall into the trap of thinking that the person you are interested in is the one that God has appointed for you.

Clive was interested in a girl, Anne. He had met her at a youth gathering. The interesting thing is that they had briefly met each other over 15 years before. However, they didn't know each other because they never kept contact in any way.

When he met Anne this time, he was interested immediately. Firstly, they had met in church. She was vegan, just like himself. Conservative, just like himself. She had a book with her that she was reading—a deeply spiritual book, which gave him a bit of an idea about her spiritual condition. She was the one. Everything that he wanted in a girl. When he made the connection about the two of them meeting all those years before, to him it looked as though this was a plan made in heaven. How could it all be coincidence? God must have allowed their paths to cross so that they could get married. "She must be God's appointed," Clive thought. What added to the situation was that Clive was at a point in his life, financially, spiritually, professionally, where he was ready for courtship. It all seemed to fit together so perfectly.

As Clive got to know Anne more and more, he found out certain things about her. Anne wasn't ready for courtship at that point—emotionally and in terms of where she was with regards to the decisions she was making for her life-work. She was not a good match for him. He was not a good match for her. Courtship was the last thing that she needed at that time. But, because he thought that she was the one that God had appointed for him, he overlooked a lot of these signals and continued in his plans to court her. He thought that because God had appointed her for him and him for her, then God would make a way for the two of them to work through all those things.

We call this behaviour "infatuation." You are interested in the person, you can see your future together, there are a lot of emotions racing through you, and you just can't seem to stop thinking about the person. When you think that a particular person is the one that God has appointed for you, you are willing to accept them with certain characteristics that will not be of benefit to you, to them, or to God's cause if you should court that person. It could be that they are not Adventist. Everything came together so beautifully and you feel that this is the person that God has appointed for you and He wants you to show them the truth. This is not God's method of matchmaking. This is not His method of evangelism. He gives us the choice, and He expects us to make the choice according to His principles.

Infatuation makes you think that the person whom you are interested in is the only one with the qualities that you want in a life-partner. It could be intelligence, experiences, beauty, skills or language. They appear to be such a brilliant package. Everything seems to fit together so perfectly and you don't think that it is possible for any other person in the entire world to fit you so "perfectly." The truth is that there is. Your current infatuation is probably not your first. You may have felt this way about many others. And each time, you didn't think that you could ever find someone like the one you were captivated by at that point.

Do not compromise God's principles because you are infatuated with a person. God will never lead you into a relationship with someone in a way that goes against the principles that He has given in His word. The person you will court is your choice. God will not "appoint" someone for you and then expect you to compromise. If you have to make a compromise, you can be sure that it was not God who appointed that person. It is more likely that Satan appointed that person for you in order to destroy you spiritually.

[Satan] is busily engaged in influencing those who are wholly unsuited to each other to unite their interests. He exults in this work, for by it he can produce more misery and hopeless woe to the human family than by exercising his skill in any other direction. Many marriages can only be productive of misery; and yet the minds of the youth run in this channel because Satan leads them there, making them believe that they must be married in order to be happy, when they have not the ability to control themselves or support a family. . .This question of marriage should be a study instead of a matter of impulse.

Letters to Young Lovers pg. 29

It may feel like you might never find another person like this one. You may not see the possibility of ever meeting someone like this person. Your heart may race. It may feel like everything that has happened in your life has prepared you for this person. But resist the pulls of infatuation. In faith, look beyond the infatuation and know that it is just temporary. Give it some time; the infatuation will die down, and you'll be infatuated with another person very soon.

You can use infatuation to your benefit. Infatuation can give you an idea of what it is that you like in a life-partner. It can also help you to see what you don't desire in a life-partner. You can use this information as you search for a suitable life-partner. Appreciate the emotional high that you get from infatuation. But don't let it cause you to make decisions that God cannot approve of. Do not compromise. Do not settle—especially on the spiritual consideration.

God's purpose for your life is a life of ministry and a life of service to Him and to humanity.

Points to Consider
I mentioned earlier that God allows us to choose whom we think best to marry. When we think things through we are making a conclusion based on information that we have collected. A necessary part of thinking is to collect information about the subject you are thinking about. So, when choosing a life-partner it is important to gather as much information as you can about a person before you conclude whether or not this person is a good match for you.

There are some characteristics about a person that you will only find out once you are actually courting that person. But, since this chapter is about looking for a potential partner, let's look at some of the things you can find out about a person without being in a one-on-one relationship with that person. It is not always necessary to be in a relationship with someone to know that the person will not be a good life-partner for you. You do not need to date around to find a good match. God has given you the ability to reason. As you do so, consider the following items.

Life and Life-work Compatibility
God's purpose for your life is a life of ministry and a life of service to Him and to humanity. This should not change in marriage. Marriage should improve your ability and efficiency in the service that you are doing. It should not make it more difficult. When you are looking for a life-partner it is important to look for someone who will fit in with the work that God has given you to do.

> Examine carefully to see if your married life would be happy, or inharmonious and wretched. Let the questions be raised, Will this union help me heavenward? Will it increase my love for God? And will it enlarge my sphere of usefulness in this life?
> *Messages to Young People* pg. 449

Marriage should make you more useful in this life. Think of your life as a car on its way to heaven. There are uphills and downhills. Think of marriage as making a modification to your car. If your marriage makes you more useful in this life, it is like adding a supercharger to your engine. This improves your speed and performance. If your marriage makes it a little bit more difficult for you to do the work that God has given you to do, it is like adding a trailer with a heavy load to your car. So when you are looking for a life-partner you will either choose a supercharger or a trailer. What will your marriage be?

The way to look at marriage is as two people joining forces in a partnership created by God in the Garden of Eden. Marriage is about a brother and sister in Christ becoming a team and ministering to each other's needs so that the world can be a better place. If they are compatible for each other and have complementary traits, this will happen. If not, one will always just be dragging the other person along.

What do I mean by a complementary marriage? If you are an engineer, for example, you are more technically inclined, so it may be wise to marry someone more on the financial side like an accountant. Or someone who is more creative and colourful, like a graphic designer. If you are a doctor, it may be beneficial to find someone also in the medical profession, such as a nurse or another doctor. If you are a plumber or a farmer, someone with more administrative skills will improve your usefulness.

There is also life compatibility. Your background, your nationality and your race need to be considered when deciding on someone to court. There are many challenges that you will face as a married couple. Avoid unnecessary challenges. It would be best to find someone that is similar in these aspects, yet complementary in others. God does not condemn inter-racial marriages, for example, but these relationships have a unique set of challenges that may be unnecessary in your situation. Remember that marriage is not about making a statement. It is about service to humanity.

Also a part of life compatibility is a consideration of your interests, your personality, your strengths and your weaknesses. Seek to find balance in these aspects. If you are more of a leading, bold person you need to find someone who is less controlling and more relaxed but with enough confidence to challenge you when you are wrong. If you are energetic, playful and sociable, you need to find someone with a steadier, calmer personality. If you are more relaxed, peaceful and laid-back, you need to find someone who is more driven and bold. All these personality traits make us who we are. However, having someone in your life that balances out your negative traits can make you more useful and efficient.

In the area of life and life-work compatibility, you will make the best decision if you already know who you are and who you are in God. This is why the time you spend as a single person is so important, and why you should only start courting once you are ready to get married.

> The young have many lessons to learn, and the most important one is to learn to know themselves.
>
> *Messages to Young People* pg. 445

Spend more time seeking to know yourself before you seek to know someone else.

You are not looking for someone who is "good enough" for you. No. You are looking for compatibility.

Spiritual Compatibility

More important than life and life-work compatibility is spiritual compatibility. Our greatest goal in life should be to make it to the Kingdom of Heaven. Whenever we make a choice we should consider how it will affect our walk with God. The person you choose to marry will have a huge effect on your spiritual life. If they are not where you are, spiritually, they will have a negative effect on your spiritual life and your eternal life will be in danger.

> The path to eternal life is steep and rugged. Take no additional weights to retard your progress.
>
> *Messages to Young People* pg. 441

In other words, don't make your journey to heaven more difficult than it already is. Think again about the trailer and the supercharger. Getting married should make you spiritually stronger than you are as a single person. "Will this union help me heavenward? Will it increase my love for God?" You are not looking for someone who is "good enough" for you. No. You are looking for compatibility.

Marriage is not about helping someone to become spiritually strong. That is what evangelism and discipleship is for. Marriage is about uniting with someone that is equally strong spiritually so that you can both be even stronger together. Whenever you are considering someone to court ask yourself whether or not your friendship with this person has brought you closer to God and strengthened your relationship with Jesus. If it has, move forward. If it has not, keep looking.

Selecting a spiritually compatible partner starts with first selecting spiritually compatible friends. The people in your life that you are the closest to will have an effect on your character and this will affect the choice that you make for someone to court.

> Be not deceived, evil communications corrupt good manners.
>
> 1 Corinthians 15:33

The dangerous thing about being deceived is that you don't know that you are being deceived until someone shows you. Paul tells us that we should not allow Satan to let us think that we will not be influenced by the corrupt characters of those with whom we spend our time.

It has been truly said, "Show me your company, and I will show you your character." The youth fail to realize how sensibly both their character and their reputation are affected by their choice of associates. One seeks the company of those whose tastes and habits and practices are congenial. He who prefers the society of the ignorant and vicious to that of the wise and good, shows that this own character is defective. His tastes and habits may at first be altogether dissimilar to the tastes and habits of those whose company he seeks; but as he mingles with this class, his thoughts and feelings change; he sacrifices right principles, and insensibly yet unavoidably sinks to the level of his companions.

Messages to Young People pgs. 411-412

Choose friends on your spiritual level or on a spiritual level that you would like to reach. This will keep you from many of the dangers that Satan has set out and it will equip you to make a good choice for a life-partner.

Physical Attraction
Physical attraction should also play a role in your consideration for someone to court. Realize that at some point, if you marry, you are actually going to have sex with this person. If you are not physically attracted to a person, you're going to have a rough marriage.

I would not be understood to mean that anyone is to marry one whom he does not love. This would be sin. But fancy and the emotional nature must not be allowed to lead on to ruin. God requires the whole heart, the supreme affections.

Messages to Young People pg. 460

The Bible also repeatedly mentions the physical beauty of the wives of the men that God favoured. Speaking of Rebekah, for example, the Bible says:

And the damsel was very fair to look upon, a virgin, neither had any man known her.

Genesis 24:16

The same is said of Sarah, Abraham's wife, Rachael, Jacob's wife, as well as other prominent women in the Bible. However, while it is necessary for you to be physically attracted to your potential life-partner, it is not the only consideration. You need to look at the whole package. Look at their character, personality, intelligence. These need to be weighed together with your physical attraction to the person. A moderately pretty girl who is strong spiritually, is a far better choice than one who is an absolute stunner, but lukewarm. Don't pass by the godly young ladies just because you are waiting for the most beautiful one.

The world places too much value on physical beauty. Usually it is artificial beauty—the makeup, the provocative clothing, Photoshop. The Christian knows that there are other things more valuable than physical beauty.

> Charm is deceptive, and beauty is fleeting; but a woman who fears the LORD is to be praised.
>
> Proverbs 31:10

It is also true that some people appear to be more physically attractive once you get to know them. Your perception of the person changes as you get to know more about their personality, and so on. You start to see this also when you look at them. This is why men can say that they are married to the most beautiful woman in the world without lying. In his eyes, a man's wife is the most beautiful woman, because when he looks at her, he does not only see her physical beauty, but he also sees her personality, her character, her spirit. You can't see it, but he can. It is a good idea to get to know someone a little bit first before you say "She's not pretty enough" or "He's not strong enough."

Providence

God is highly interested in our lives. That is why He seeks a personal relationship with each and every one of us. The subject of courtship is also very important to Him because He is our Father. When searching for a life-partner, keep God in the loop of things, and continuously seek His will. God, by His Providence, will bring people into your life and will direct circumstances to move a certain way as He helps you to find a suitable life-partner.

In the introduction of this book, I told the story of a young lady that I met during my first year at university, Alexandra. I'm going to give you more details about how we met in order to demonstrate to you how deeply interested God is in helping us find a suitable partner, and how He acts in our lives through His Divine Providence.

The story actually starts with another young lady, Maria. I met Maria during high school. Maria was a very attractive girl, and she had a stunning personality as well. We had a lot in common, we could talk well together, and I could make her laugh much easier than most other guys could. I really enjoyed spending time with her, and I could see that she enjoyed spending time with me too.

The social pressures of high school made me think twice about getting into a relationship with her at that time. I had come out of a relationship just over a year before and she had come out of a relationship a few months before. It didn't seem right. Although she wanted to be in a relationship with me, and I wanted to be in a relationship with her, I told her that we should remain friends for a while. We completed high school and started university. Now, without the social pressures of high school I felt that we were in a better position to start dating.

Sometime between the tenth grade and the end of high school I had become a more keen reader. The first book that I can honestly say I read from cover to cover was the book "Steps to Christ." Reading became a very important part of my life and my walk with God. In my first year of university I was reading a book on love and relationships by a very well-known Seventh-day Adventist Christian author. The book gave me a lot of insight into love and relationships; it was a good read.

As I was reading the book, I got the impression that Maria would be a good person for me to date. Notice that I said "date." The book made no reference to Biblical courtship, it spoke nothing of preparing for your life-work before getting into a relationship, and it spoke nothing of marrying within the church. Although the book was written by a Seventh-day Adventist author, the author encouraged the dating procedure that is practiced in the world. Obviously I cannot remember every detail of the book. But, like I said, the conclusion that I came to after reading that book was that I should start dating Maria.

There were a few problems with that. Maria was not Adventist, and so we had a different belief system and different values. We liked each other though, and we enjoyed each other's company. If we had dated, with time, I suppose, she may have come to know the Adventist truth and decided to follow. But this is not what relationships are for. Also, the risk there would be that I may have become weaker as an Adventist and perhaps followed her. Or maybe I would have stayed in the Adventist church and become a lukewarm benchwarmer. Looking back on the situation, I see now what great danger I was in of making a shipwreck of my faith.

Maria and I had not yet completed preparation for our life-work, we had barely started preparation. This was not something that my Father in heaven would have wanted. But I didn't know these things at that time. I decided in my heart that I was going to ask Maria to date me. We were still keeping contact, so I knew that she still liked me and would agree to dating. It was a Friday afternoon that I came to this conclusion and I spoke to God about my decision to date Maria. I told Him that, from what I had read, this seemed like a good move to make. I ended my conversation with God by saying, "But, Lord, if it is not your will, please change my mind."

The following day, a Sabbath day, Alexandra walked into my life. We were having a youth day celebration at church, so the church had invited many people from other Seventh-day Adventist churches to come and join in. Alexandra was there with her family. I was impressed from the moment I saw her. She was dressed really well—with taste and modesty, as Adventist girls should be dressed. I got to speaking to her and she told me that she was in her last year of high school and that she was planning to go into medicine and perhaps study at Loma Linda University. My hope of course was that she would come to my university and study medicine there. But, that's beside the point. The point is that my mind was changed.

As I mentioned in the introduction, Alexandra was not interested in me. That was not important from my heavenly Father's perspective. All He needed to do to prevent me from getting into a relationship with Maria was to show me that girls like Alexandra did exist. Devoted, attractive, Adventist young girls, with a love for truth, a love for God, and a desire to do His work. I just needed to meet Alexandra to realize that I was making a mistake by seeking to date Maria.

In Isaac's situation, God's Providence was also there in helping to find a suitable life-partner for him. Remember Eliezer's prayer,

And let it come to pass, that the damsel to whom I shall say, Let down thy pitcher, I pray thee, that I may drink; and she shall say, Drink, and I will give thy camels drink also: let the same be she that thou hast appointed for thy servant Isaac; and thereby shall I know that thou hast showed kindness unto my master.

Genesis 24:14

The Bible tells us that before Eliezer had even finished praying, his prayer was being answered. Notice also, that although his prayer was answered, it was also important that Rebekah was from the right family. It was not just about fulfilling the sign, but also about Rebekah being family of Abraham. Eliezer only praised God for giving him success after he found out that Rebekah was related to Abraham. The sign was important, but more important was the instruction from Abraham that the young lady be family—of the same faith, in other words.

God is interested in the choices that we make when it comes to relationships. If you are seeking the will of God, if you are following the principles that He has shown you already, and you are allowing Him to play an active role in your life in this area, and in all other areas of your life, you will see His Providence. It may not be in the same way that God showed Eliezer that Rebekah was the right woman for Isaac. God's Providence in your life may be very different, but God will show you what He needs to show you in the way that you need it to be shown to you. And when He speaks, listen.

I must also mention that God will not show you to do something that goes against the principles that He has given in His word. God does not work like that. He gives us guidance from His word and if, while following that guidance, He feels we need some extra help, He will perform a miracle in our lives. Yes, there are exceptions, but be careful not to be presumptuous in thinking that you are the exception just because you have romantic feelings for someone.

Counselling
Solomon writes in the book of Proverbs:

Where no counsel is, the people fall: but in the multitude of counsellers there is safety.

Proverbs 11:14

When deciding on a person to court it is not wise to make the decision all

Total surrender is needed when searching for a life-partner.

by yourself. God has placed experienced men and women in your life that can give you guidance. Seek counsel from them. Tell them how you feel. Tell them what you think. Listen to their counsel. It is not necessary for you to follow everything that they say. But listen to what they have to say and decide whether or not what they say is in line with the word of God. Use what is good. Reject what is not.

Speaking to Your Parents

In the dating procedure, parents usually get involved long after the relationship has started. This is not God's way. Speaking of relationships, Ellen White writes:

> When will our youth be wise? How long will this kind of work go on? Shall children consult only their own desires and inclinations, irrespective of the advice and judgment of their parents? Some seem never to bestow a thought upon their parents' wishes or preferences, nor to regard their matured judgment. Selfishness has closed the door of their hearts to filial affection. The minds of the young need to be aroused in regard to this matter. The fifth commandment is the only commandment to which is annexed a promise; but it is held lightly, and is even positively ignored by the lover's claim.
>
> *Messages to Young People* pg. 448

I deeply regret the relationships that I got into without my parents knowing. When I was growing up, I had no one to tell me that it was wrong to have a relationship without your parents knowing. The examples that I had seen made me think that it was the normal way of doing things. This kind of thinking is very dangerous and it is the way Satan wants it. He tries to prevent us from getting the wisdom of our parents so that he can ruin our lives. Your parents should always know what is happening in your life, especially when it comes to relationships.

Relationships involve a lot of feelings and emotions. We need wise counsellors that can look at the situation from the outside, without the feelings, and help us see what is really going on, what we are getting ourselves into and what the facts are. When we get involved in relationships we tend to get our heart involved very quickly, it becomes difficult to think clearly, and it becomes difficult to see the hard truth. We tend to overlook certain things that are important because of our feelings for the person. If our parents are not involved from the start and we develop strong bonds for someone whom we should not, we tend to see our parents as nuisances interrupting our relationship experience and not as wise counsellors helping us to find the right person. And Satan rejoices.

Melissa was one of the most beautiful girls that Lewis had ever come across. They had been friends for a long time and it seemed as though she was interested in being in a relationship with him. Lewis knew that he would be violating God's principles if he had to be in a relationship with her. She was not baptized, meaning that she had not fully decided to follow Jesus. Lewis had been baptized in his early teens and was a faithful church member. But Melissa was so beautiful, and she liked him. He decided that, because he had some influence with her, he would try to assist her in making a decision for Christ. Perhaps if she was baptized things might be a little different and they could perhaps court.

Lewis would call Melissa sometimes and they would talk for an hour at a time. Sometimes about spiritual things, but mostly about everything else. The more they talked, the more Lewis felt as though their feelings for each other were growing deeper and deeper. Lewis began to realize that he was not thinking properly. He was placing his feelings ahead of God's leading. He began to realize that he was spending a lot of time day dreaming about what their future life would be like together. On the one hand Lewis felt that he was leading Melissa to Christ. On the other hand, he could see that he was deeply infatuated.

Lewis was a bit confused and he knew that he needed guidance. He called a meeting with his parents, uncle, aunt and two other family members that he trusted. He explained to them what was happening. He told them how he felt. They gave him sound advice. They were able to look at the situation without the feelings that he had. They helped him to see the danger that he was in by developing a close relationship with someone not committed to Christ. They prayed about it, and in the next few days Lewis was able to see more clearly the danger that he was in and he decided that it would be best to pull back a little bit on the friendship. Praise God for godly family members!

God has placed men and women in your life to guide you and to teach you. They may not be perfect, but it is not necessary for a counsellor to be perfect for them to give good counsel. Ask for advice from those who love you. Get wisdom from your pastor, your family members and your friends. Don't try to do it all by yourself just because you have strong feelings for someone. Your parents should be the first people that you go to whenever you feel that you are being drawn into a close relationship with someone. And if they are godly, all the more reason to do so. No one on earth cares about your happiness as much as they do.

Speaking to God

Greater even than the love of your parents is the love of God for you. Greater than your parents' desire for your happiness is the desire of God for your happiness. Not only should we speak to our parents about the relationships that we are developing, but we should also speak to God.

> If men and women are in the habit of praying twice a day before they contemplate marriage, they should pray four times a day when such a step is anticipated. Marriage is something that will influence and affect your life, both in this world and in the world to come. A sincere Christian will not advance his plans in this direction without the knowledge that God approves his course.
>
> *Messages to Young People* pg. 460

Our prayers should be equal to the size of the task. The bigger the task, the more time we should spend speaking to God about it. Marriage, as the statement says, affects the rest of our lives as well as our life in heaven. Choosing someone to marry is one of the greatest tasks we will ever face. We should pray accordingly.

Prayer, it has been said, does not bring God down to us. Rather, it lifts us up to God. Speaking to God increases our faith, it helps us to realize how weak we are as human beings, and it teaches us to surrender our will to God. We need the mind of God as we search for a life-partner. We need wisdom from God as we search for a life-partner. And our loving Father gives these gifts to us freely if we ask for them in prayer. But we must ask.

Total surrender is needed when searching for a life-partner. Many attractive paths will be placed before you. Each offering their own set of pleasures. But many of these attractive paths lead to a bad choice in a life-partner. Daily prayer and devotion to God will allow you to set your affections on things above and not on things on the earth that you may know and do what is good and acceptable in the eyes of God; that you may make a choice that will bring joy and happiness in this life and in the next. Do not neglect private prayer as you seek a life-partner.

The Search

We do not actively search for life-partners today in the way that we should. In the Bible we find Abraham sending his trusted servant to a faraway land to find a wife for his son Isaac. We find Jacob also travelling to a faraway land, Padan Aram, to his mother's relatives to find a wife. Good life-partners are not always found in your immediate surroundings, at your local church, in your conference, or at work. Good life-partners are not likely to just show up in your life one day. You have to make a decided effort to go and look for someone.

Solomon tells us in the book of Proverbs:

> The man who finds a wife finds a treasure, and he receives favour from the Lord.
>
> Proverbs 18:22 (NLT)

Jesus said in Matthew 7:7 that it is in seeking that we find. Solomon continues with his metaphor of a treasure and further tells us:

> Who can find a virtuous wife? For her worth is far above rubies.
>
> Proverbs 31:10 (NKJV)

Rubies do not lay on the surface of the earth. It is very rare that you will one day bump into a ruby while strolling in a park. Rubies have to be mined. You have to go to the right place, where rubies are found. You have to search through the rubble. Only then do you find a ruby. The same is true in finding a suitable life-partner. You must go where they can be found and actively search through the rubble until you find one. If you do not go out looking for a ruby, you are not likely to find one.

The average church person does not want to take great effort to look for a life-partner. The average person is willing to settle for someone in their local congregation or district and live an average life with that person when God has called them to great things. For them, it is too much work to go out looking. Jacob's journey was over 600 km. Without a car. How far are you willing to travel to search for a life-partner? How much value do you place on finding a suitable life-partner. Solomon gives us the true value of the task: far above the price of rubies.

Modern technology has made it easier for us to make an active search. Today, you can travel the distance that Jacob travelled in less than half a day. Yet, people are still willing to settle for someone who lives down the road. The internet has made it possible for us to meet and befriend people in faraway countries from the comfort of our own homes. We do not use these tools to our benefit as much as we should, and the Kingdom of God suffers because we are poorly mated. We were too lazy and not creative enough to find suitable life-partners.

If we do not make an effort to do a proper search to find a compatible life-partner, Satan is ready to match us up with someone whom he knows will ruin our walk with God. If we just sit around hoping that we will bump into the right person, Satan may cause us to bump into the wrong person. He is in the matchmaking business:

> [Satan] is busily engaged in influencing those who are wholly unsuited to each other to unite their interests. He exults in this work, for by it he can produce more misery and hopeless woe to the human family than by exercising his skill in any other direction.
>
> *Letters to Young Lovers* pg. 29

Furthermore, parents do not fully realize their God-given responsibility of finding a life-partner for their son or daughter. Parents should not just sit back and hope that their son or daughter meets the right person. Fathers and mothers should be like Abraham who sends his servant to go look for a wife. They should be like Naomi who instructs Ruth to go down to the threshing floor where Boaz will notice her. Parents should place their sons and daughters where they will develop friendships and bonds with godly young men and women. Dating puts the responsibility of finding a suitable life-partner in the hands of the children, but in reality it is the responsibility of the parents, with input from the children.

Fathers and mothers should feel that a duty devolves upon them to guide the affections of the youth, that they may be placed upon those who will be suitable companions. They should feel it a duty, by their own teaching and example, with the assisting grace of God, to so mold the character of the children from their earliest years that they will be pure and noble and will be attracted to the good and true. Like attracts like; like appreciates like. Let the love for truth and purity and goodness be early implanted in the soul, and the youth will seek the society of those who possess these characteristics.

Patriarchs and Prophets pg. 176

Parents should meet up with other parents who have sons and daughters of similar age. They should befriend them with the intention of finding compatible life-partners for their sons and daughters. And it should be taken seriously. They should sit down with other parents and discuss the potential for marriage. It should not be left to chance. One of the reasons that parents often do not approve of the person that their son or daughter brings home is that they did not make any effort to help their son or daughter find a good life-partner. The young people then take it into their own hands and make a foolish choice.

When meeting other young people, play an active role in organizing wholesome group activities. Plan to go horse-riding together, or on a picnic on a mountainside. Go on hiking trips. Plan outreach or community service activities together. Be creative. The possibilities are infinite when you apply your mind to actively seek to meet and to get to know other young people. From this network of friends that you create you may be able to find and select a suitable life-partner.

Do not be in a hurry to get married. Take your time as you get to know other singles. Also, when you meet someone, do not immediately decide whether or not they are a good match for you. Take time to get to know the person. And if they need some assistance in their walk with God, help them along. Pray for them and with them. Give them a book to read, or some audio to listen to. This can be very profitable later on in life. You do not know if this person may one day come back into your life and, as a result of your ministry to them, be the spiritually strong life-partner that you are looking for. Or, you may be preparing them to become a suitable partner for someone else that might meet them further along the way.

However, always be motivated by your desire to benefit them and not yourself.

Cast your bread upon the waters,
For you will find it after many days.
In the morning sow your seed,
And in the evening do not withhold your hand;
For you do not know which will prosper,
Either this or that,
Or whether both alike will be good.

Ecclesiastes 11:1, 6

Actively search for someone to court, spend time in prayer, speak to your parents and speak to your loved ones. Make friends with a lot of singles and find out as much about them as possible without committing to a one-on-one relationship. Look at each person's character, their interests, their background, their life-work. Most importantly, look for spiritual compatibility. Discuss with your parents what you have read in this chapter and decide with them whether or not you are ready to begin the search for a life-partner. If you are ready, start making plans as to how you will go about the search.

As you weigh the characters and personalities of those whom you meet and develop friendships with, you may narrow down the possibilities to maybe one or two people. Spend time in prayer and in consultation with those whom you love and who love you. Seek the will of God. Ask Him what you should do. Examine each person's character as much as you can. Speak also to people who know the person well. Do a proper investigation. And only when you have learned all that you possibly can learn about them outside of a one-on-one relationship, and God has shown you to move forward, proceed to the next step.

In the next chapter we will look at what needs to take place to set up the courtship. What are the roles of the young man and young lady involved? What roles do the parents play? All these will be addressed as we explore the next step in the courtship procedure.

Summary

Man is a social being, just as God is. Getting married allows men and women to enjoy together the blessings that God has given to the human race. These include material blessings, as well as the blessings of love, sharing, and companionship. Getting married allows us to grow spiritually and in character, it allows us to have someone who can help balance our strengths and weakness, it makes us better able to do the work that God has given us to do, and it gives us the framework in which we can experience the gift of sexual intimacy.

God has given each person the choice of whether or not to get married, when to get married, and whom to get married to. Generally, there is not one special person appointed for you. God has given you the freedom to choose who you think best to marry. He has given principles in His word upon which you can make your choice. Life and life-work compatibility, spiritual compatibility, physical attraction, and providence are all to be considered when we make this choice.

When searching for a person to court, young people should consult with their parents, the pastor, other family members and whoever else they feel has their best interest at heart. It should not be done alone. Young people should spend a great amount of time in prayer while they are considering individuals as possible life-partners. They should study the character of the person in whom they have interest, and should consult with people that know the individual well.

Ultimately, it is the responsibility of a young man and young lady's parents to ensure that they find suitable life-partners. Parents and young people together should conduct an active search for a potential life-partner to court.

Chapter Three

Asking Dad

_____

"Honour thy father and thy mother: that thy days may be long upon the land which the LORD thy God giveth thee."

Exodus 20:12

Asking Dad

At this point we need to look at the family structure given in the Bible. Whether you are a boy or a girl, you can play an active role in searching for a suitable life-partner. However, there are fundamental differences between the roles that young men, young ladies, and their respective parents are to play in starting courtship. The Bible gives us guidance about these differences. In this chapter we will look at how to go about setting up the courtship once you have decided, along with your guardians, that a particular person is the one that you should court.

Young woman, you are not your own. You are a gift from God to your parents.

Dad

The Bible gives a very special role to the father of a young woman. Have you ever wondered why during a wedding ceremony a young lady's dad will walk her down the aisle, give her a kiss and then present her to the man she is marrying? Have you ever wondered why during a wedding ceremony the minister asks "Who gives this this woman to be married to this man?" It all has to do with the responsibility and authority that God has given the father of a woman.

Young woman, you are not your own. You are a gift from God to your parents. They are responsible to ensure that you make it to the Kingdom of Heaven, and part of that responsibility involves guarding and preserving your virginity until marriage. It is therefore your dad's responsibility to ensure that you court only good, godly, Christian men. He has the highest authority when it comes to the courtship process. Take a look at this verse in the book of 1 Corinthians. It is speaking about a father—"the man"—and his daughter—"his virgin":

> But if any man thinks he is behaving improperly toward his virgin, if she is past the flower of youth, and thus it must be, let him do what he wishes. He does not sin; let them marry. Nevertheless he who stands steadfast in his heart, having no necessity, but has power over his own will, and has so determined in his heart that he will keep his virgin, does well. So then he who gives her in marriage does well, but he who does not give her in

marriage does better.

1 Corinthians 7:36-38 (NKJV)

Due to the persecution that the Corinthians are facing, Paul is telling the Corinthians that it may not be wise to marry. As he does this, he makes mention of the father's authority over his daughter, that it is his decision whether or not she should be given in marriage. Notice this principle also appearing in these other passages in the Bible:

And [Tamar, the daughter in law of Judah,] put her widow's garments off from her, and covered her with a vail, and wrapped herself, and sat in an open place, which is by the way to Timnath; for she saw that Shelah was grown, and she was not given unto him to wife.

Genesis 38:14

And they took their daughters to be their wives, and gave their daughters to their sons, and served their gods.

Judges 3:6

The fire consumed their young men; and their maidens were not given to marriage.

Psalm 78:63

Sons marry and daughters are given in marriage. And God has given the responsibility to the father to decide which is best for his daughter. I am not sure if this was in God's original design, or if it was a result of the fall that the woman is subject to her father before she is married and then subject to her husband once she is married. We do notice, however, in the creation account in the book of Genesis, that God, the father of both Adam and Eve, brings Eve to Adam and gives her to him in marriage.

It is also the father's responsibility to ensure that the one whom his daughter is marrying is suitable for her, that he can and will take care of her physical needs, emotional needs, financial needs and, most importantly, her spiritual needs, in the same way that he, her father, has been taking care of these needs. Thus, he has the right and the solemn responsibility to refuse a suitor who does not meet God's standards of a potential husband. If he does not exercise this responsibility, he is accountable to God for allowing the ruin of his daughter if it should come to that. Young ladies, do not look at this as a restriction to your happiness, but rather as a protection of that happiness. Praise God if you have a father who will turn away young men who do not meet God's standards when it comes to the responsibility of a Christian husband.

A girl's dad is the guardian of her heart. Dad can ask the serious questions that a girl may be too shy to ask. Questions like, "Do you have a job?" "Are you baptized?" He can do an investigation, in a friendly manner, without scaring off the young man. He can help to arrange a get-together with the young man's parents if he wishes. These questions and considerations will prevent the young lady's heart from being broken by a relationship that does not end well, or by a relationship that is not leading towards a marriage proposal.

A godly Christian father will also know that he is not looking for perfection in a young man. Rather, he is looking at the general trend of the young man's life, evidence of some kind of understanding of the duties and responsibilities of a Christian husband and father, and evidence of a desire to love and to please God above all else.

Marriage is about family, not just about the couple involved.

A young man who enjoys the society and wins the friendship of a young lady unknown to her parents, does not act a noble Christian part toward her or toward her parents. . . Marriages contracted under such influences are not according to the word of God. "Thou shalt not steal," was written by the finger of God upon the tables of stone; yet how much underhand stealing is practiced and excused.

Messages to Young People pg. 445

Marriage is about family, not just about the couple involved. Family should be there from the start, helping, guiding and assisting the courtship process. The many silly jokes about bad in-laws and extended family are inappropriate. The jokes give an idea of the challenges that couples face in getting along with the family of their partner. These challenges are unnecessary and are not a true reflection of what God wants for a couple. They are the result of marriages formed through the world's dating procedure and not on God's courtship principles.

Once a young lady's father is satisfied that the young man is a suitable candidate to court his daughter he can allow the young man to court his daughter. Yet, she still has the choice as to whether or not she would like a courtship with the young man. In the story of Isaac and Rebekah, we find that Rebekah was asked whether or not she would go to become Isaac's wife. She made the decision to go.

In my high school days I dated a girl, Daniela. The sweetest girl ever. I asked her to go out with me while walking back to class with her after lunch break at school one day. She said "Yes" and about a week and a half later we went on our first date. We had good times together. We experienced all the emotions, the thrills, and the excitement that comes from dating in high school. We talked for hours on the phone. She usually was the one calling me because her father had some sort of business at home that allowed them unlimited time to use the phone.

My parents never knew about Daniela. On our first date I lied to my parents telling them that I would be going out with some friends. Some of my cousins knew, though. They were quite happy for me that I was in a relationship with someone. It seemed like this was the way things ought to be done: keep it a secret from your parents and only introduce them when it becomes really serious. I could even rely on some of my cousins to help me with some money so that I could take Daniela on a date. Money is hard to come by when you are a high school student, and the dating scene requires quite a bit of it.

I don't think Daniela's parents knew about us either. If her parents were picking her up, for example, we would say good-bye inside the mall or the place where we went for our date, and she would go by herself to her parents' car.

Daniela was not Adventist; she grew up Catholic. She also felt that it was acceptable to drink alcohol and to smoke. But, what is really interesting is that although we were from different religious backgrounds and had a different set of values, we both knew the dating procedure well. Boy meets girl and they like each other. Boy asks girl on a date and she accepts. Dating happens often and physical intimacy is normal. Parents are not involved at all until at some point when you decide to tell them, or they find out somehow. We followed it perfectly, without even thinking about it.

About two and a half months after we had started dating, my feelings started to change. I no longer enjoyed being in a relationship with her. I was looking at some of the other girls in the school and the one that I was with just wasn't doing it for me anymore. Daniela could sense that something was wrong, so she asked me about it. I brushed it off; I told her we'd talk some other time. In my heart I was planning to break up with her. I was just waiting for the right time. The right time did come, during break time one day, shortly before the bell rang to mark the end of break. My words to her were "I don't feel the same way about you anymore."

Daniela walked away, not slowly, with her face slightly to the ground and trying to keep from crying. Some of our friends, girls and boys, watched the whole thing. Daniela walked to one of our mutual friends, Amy. Amy grabbed Daniela to give her a hug, and as she did Daniela burst into tears. I broke her heart. To this day I deeply regret breaking her heart. She did not deserve to be hurt like that. She did not deserve to be treated that way. I walked away. The bell rang and it was time to get back to class.

Two principles may have prevented the hurt that I caused Daniela. Firstly, if she had requested that I speak to her parents before dating her we may never actually have dated. Alternatively, if I had known that parents are to be involved from the beginning, I would have spoken to my parents about my interest in Daniela. They would have given me sound advice and I probably never would have dated Daniela. Or, suppose my dad said "Go for it!" I may then have gone to her parents, told them I wanted to date their daughter, they would have asked me if I had a job and, once again, we may never have dated.

Secondly, if I had acted from principle instead of from feeling I also would not have broken her heart. I may never have asked her out because I would have reasoned that being in a relationship was not the right thing to do because, one, we were not ready for relationships—we were still in school—two, we were not compatible in terms of our religious backgrounds and values, and, three, I was keeping it a secret from my parents.

Acting from feeling instead of principle is the cause of heartbreak in relationships.

Even in dating, I may have prevented the hurt. I could have reasoned that I had to push past my change in feelings for her, and instead loved her, cared for her, and treated her the way a woman should be treated. But I didn't. I acted based on my feelings, and I hurt her feelings. I could also have allowed her to dump me. But I wasn't man enough to take a blow to my ego like that. What would the guys say? What would it do to my reputation with all the other girls? My reputation was more important than the feelings of another human being. I was more important than her. I loved myself more than I loved my neighbour.

Acting from feeling instead of principle is the cause of heartbreak in relationships. Acting out of feelings instead of principle is the cause of divorce. The dating procedure and the romance that forms a big part of the procedure make it nearly impossible to act from principle instead of feeling and impulse. A life of dating prepares you to make decisions based on feelings and impulse. Thus, it prepares you for divorce due to feelings and perhaps even divorce from Christ based on feelings and impulse.

Ladies, if you are ever approached by a young man who wants to be in a relationship with you, ask him if you can sit down together to speak to your parents. If the man is serious about evaluating your compatibility for marriage, he will do this. If he is not willing to speak to your parents, he will just waste your time. It's not worth it to be in a relationship with someone who just wants to hang out. By being in a relationship that is not a means of determining your compatibility for marriage, you become unavailable to the really serious guys, and your happiness in this life and in the next are in danger. Let him speak to your dad, whether privately, with you present, or even a family to family discussion. You have more to gain than to lose.

To summarise then, in the courtship procedure, a young man approaches the parents, or his parents are to approach the parents, of the young lady he wishes to court. The young lady's parents, especially her father, will decide whether or not to allow the courtship to take place. If they do allow it, then the young lady will decide whether or not she would like to court the young man. If a father seeks to give his daughter in marriage to a particular young man, he may then, with his daughter's consent, also approach the young man's parents, or the young man, to set up courtship. A young lady may also let her parents know of someone that she sees to be a good potential life-partner and her parents can approach him or his parents as well.

The main principle in this step of the courtship procedure is that parents are aware of what is taking place. Relationships should not be a secret. The specifics of how you achieve this are not as important as the principle itself. Let your parents know what is taking place in your life when it comes to members of the opposite sex. Trust their guidance and their wisdom. Trust that they love you and want only the best for you.

> The main principle in this step of the courtship procedure is that parents are aware of what is taking place.

The Counselling Continues
From whichever side the courtship proposal comes, whether it is the father or parents of the young lady coming to the parents of a young man to request a courtship, or if it is the young man or his parents coming to the parents of the young lady to request courtship, there will probably be some sort of surprise, unless the person has shown their interest before the courtship request. That's fine. How do you suppose Rebekah felt when she was suddenly asked, "Will you go with this man?" When she woke up that morning, she probably had no idea that before the end of the day she would be faced with the choice of leaving home to be married to some man she hadn't even met.

Let's suppose that it is the young lady's parents who have been approached. Let's also suppose that the young lady is unaware of the young man's interest. If the parents have approved of the young man, they inform the young lady of the request in their own time. Young lady, it is now your turn to get some counselling. It is now your turn to do some research on the character of the young man. Ask questions about his background, speak to people who know him well, speak to your parents, your loved ones, your pastor, tell them how you see the matter and ask them for guidance. Most of all spend those extra moments in prayer seeking the will and guidance of God.

This may be a shock to you, but remember that if he has taken the time to speak to your parents, or if his parents have spoken to your parents, he has in all likelihood spent a lot of time evaluating your character, counselled with his parents and spent a great deal of time on his knees. It is not an easy matter to approach a young lady's dad. I know, I've been there. It makes you want to make doubly and triply sure that what you are doing is the will of God. And if he has come to this point, he is sure that this is what God wants him to do.

In any case, the choice is still yours. You are not forced to accept his request just because he asked. My point here is just that you give his request the consideration that it deserves. Take your time. Do not be in a hurry to make a decision for or against the request:

> Weigh every sentiment and watch every development of character in the one with whom you think to unite your life destiny.
> *Letters to Young Lovers* pg. 90

Consult your feelings, but remember that feelings are not the main thing. The dating procedure puts feelings at the forefront and decisions are made mostly on the basis of feeling instead of on the principles of God's Kingdom. Courtship allows you to take things slowly, to think clearly and to consider all points without the noise and the rush of the emotions. Consider how you feel, but let your desire to honour God and to make it to the Kingdom of Heaven be your first priority. Enjoy the breathing space that courtship allows for. Once you have made your decision, let your parents know and then inform the young man. If you are a young man and it was you or your parents who were approached by the young lady's parents, let your parents know your decision and then inform the young lady and her parents.

In Not-so-Ideal Situations
We live in an imperfect world, and so I imagine that there may be someone reading this book that does not have godly parents who can take the role that parents should in this important part of the courtship process. If that is you, then you may consider finding a godly couple in your church family that can perform this function for you. Pray about it and choose a couple that you feel most comfortable with to be your spiritual parents or guardians. If you do not have a father in your life, but you have a godly mother she too may take on the role that your father would have taken.

Young lady if you do not have anyone in your life to perform the role of the father, I urge you not to approach a young man directly to request courtship. You may put yourself where he may notice you. But if he does not have enough initiative or interest in you to initiate courtship, it really is not worth it for you to take the lead in a relationship such as this.

In some cases, the situation may call for the young man to indicate his interest and intentions to a young lady before or without meeting her parents. For whatever reason, her parents might not be accessible. Still, a young lady should take her time as she considers the request and meet with her guardians or parents to discuss the request, whether with the young man, or without him.

The principle once again is that you don't do things all by yourself and that you consult those older and wiser than yourself, and those that have a vested interest in your life, as you move into a one-on-one relationship with someone. Whatever your specific circumstance is, surrender yourself to God and take your plans to Him in prayer, seek His will and He will show you what to do. Keep the principle in mind. The specifics will become clear if you let God lead.

Summary
A young lady is under the authority of her father while she is still single. It is his responsibility to guard and preserve her virginity until she is married. This ensures a hedge of protection around the young lady and prevents her from being led astray by immoral young men. A young lady's parents should be consulted if a young man desires to court the young lady. Similarly a young man's parents should be consulted if a young lady's parents, along with the young lady's consent, desire to give their daughter to him in marriage. Courtship begins when each party agrees that they are willing to court.

Chapter Four

Get a Chaperone

"Promise me, O women of Jerusalem, by the gazelles and wild deer, not to awaken love until the time is right."

Song of Solomon 2:7 (NLT)

Get a Chaperone

The courting process is about becoming well acquainted with the person you are courting so that you can make an informed decision about whether or not this person is a suitable match for you to get married to. In this chapter we discuss what should and should not take place during courtship so that this goal achieved. Guys, even if it was you or your parents who were approached by the young lady's parents, take the lead in courtship. As a man, you will be the leader of your home one day. Courtship gives you the opportunity to practice that leadership capability.

Chaper-what?
A chaperone is an adult who goes with young unmarried people on social occasions. The chaperone's job is to prevent young people from doing inappropriate things, like getting physically intimate with each other.

When you are courting someone make sure that you are never completely alone with that person. Ask an adult, like a parent, an aunt or an uncle, or a married couple to be present when you might find yourself alone somewhere. Visit public places when you go out, or spend your time where there are other people close by. There are some things that you will not do in the presence of other people, like getting physical—kissing, fondling, rubbing, taking clothes off and so on.

You are sexually attracted to the person that you are courting. If you were not, you would not be courting them. Two people left alone who are physically attracted to each other, and each knows that the other is physically attracted to them, are in a dangerous situation if they are not yet married. Satan will do everything in his power to get them to commit fornication. If he succeeds, it can lead to a ruined marriage, if they do get married. If you have a chaperone or if you are in a public setting, this temptation is greatly reduced. Paul tells us that we should not put ourselves in a position where we can sin:

> But put ye on the Lord Jesus Christ, and make not provision for the flesh, to fulfil the lusts thereof.
>
> Romans 13:14

The courtship process is a time to get to know the person you are courting on an intellectual, emotional and spiritual level.

For example, don't meet up alone at your uncle's house if they are out of town for the weekend. Of course, it is wise also to discuss these boundaries with the person whom you are courting so that you both know where the boundaries are.

Courting is not like dating, where you go out simply for entertainment. Courtship is about getting to know the person you are courting. You may participate in innocent socially pleasurable activities as a means of getting to know each other, but these are not the main thing. So, for most of the time you spend together you will probably be around each other's families and friends. The best place to get to know someone is in their parents' home. At home, you are less likely to be in a situation where you can fall into the temptation of getting physical. You are also more likely to see who the person really is.

The courtship process is a time to get to know the person you are courting on an intellectual, emotional and spiritual level. As soon as you become intimate with that person on a physical level, you change the focus of the relationship from a research process to a romantic game. When you see each other, your desire is no longer to determine whether this person is the right person for you to marry as much as it is about getting physically intimate. It also ruins your judgment of the other person's character. It is important to keep the focus of the relationship on finding out whether or not the person you are courting is the one that you should marry.

The person or people that are with you and around you when you are together do not have to hear what you are saying to each other. They can just be close by, or perhaps in the next room, so that you do not have any temptation to get physical. However, they must be responsible people. In the previous chapter we spoke about the father of a girl being responsible to guard and preserve the virginity of his daughter. Parents should also take responsibility and encourage their sons and daughters to exercise great caution in this area.

Courtship should be openly announced. Everyone that you love, your friends, your family, everyone should be aware that you are courting. It should not be a secret. When people see you and the person that you are courting walking alone somewhere, they should not have to guess what is going on. They should know that the two of you are courting. Friends and family can also keep you both in prayer as you decide on whether or not you are suited for each other.

Another reason for having a supervised courtship is to protect your reputation, especially if you are a young lady. People are likely to assume that because you are in a relationship with someone and you spend time together completely alone you are getting physically involved. This gives you a reputation as a promiscuous person with loose morals. People might not say it to you face, but they may be thinking it, and they may talk about you to other people. However, if you make it a rule for yourselves always to be in the presence of a cautioning adult, such scandals need not arise. The wise man says,

> Choose a good reputation over great riches; being held in high esteem is better than silver or gold.
>
> Proverbs 22:1 (NLT)

It is not only your reputation that needs to be protected but also the reputation of the church of God. We are surrounded by witnesses from all walks of life and they are looking at how Christians behave and at how Seventh-day Adventists behave. They are making a judgment on the church of God and the God of the church. As ambassadors of God's Kingdom, we need to conduct ourselves in a manner that is honourable to God. As Christians, we need to protect our reputations because we are representing Christ.

In courtship, spend time getting to know each other on a day-to-day level. Courtship is not just about having fun together; it is about becoming well acquainted with who this person is. It is a time to find out how this person solves problems, how close they are to God, what value they place on household responsibilities, what their views are on doctrinal and philosophical issues. These things, and many more, you will find out by spending time with them around the home, at church, while working (if this is possible), and other everyday activities. Not by going on dates.

As you become closer to the person that you are courting, you will become more comfortable with sharing certain things with them. Open up. Let them get to know you as you get to know them. When you feel comfortable, talk about the past, talk about mistakes that you have made, lessons you have learned, hardships, victories, things that made you sad, things that made you happy.

Physical Affection
Physical affection is not appropriate before marriage. What do I mean by physical affection? I'm talking about kissing, holding, rubbing, long hugs and yes, even hand holding in some instances. Physical affection is anything that will cause sexual arousal. This does differ from person to person though. Notice what Paul says to the Corinthians:

> Now concerning the things of which you wrote to me: It is good for a man not to touch a woman. Nevertheless, because of sexual immorality, let each man have his own wife, and let each woman have her own husband. Let the husband render to his wife the affection due her, and likewise also the wife to her husband.
>
> 1 Corinthians 7:1-3

Touching someone in a sexual way is reserved for people who are married. There is something deeply psychological that happens inside the human brain when two people show physical affection to each other. It causes a strong bond between the couple that becomes hard to break. The reason why we don't need this bond during courtship is that you do not know yet if this person is the one that you are going to get married to. If they are not, it will be hard to end the courtship if you have gotten to know them on a physical level. Let's look at another text:

> Let thy fountain be blessed: and rejoice with the wife of thy youth. Let her be as the loving hind and pleasant roe; let her breasts satisfy thee at all times; and be thou ravished always with her love.
>
> Proverbs 5:18-19

This is Solomon speaking and he speaks about breast fondling as something that a man does with his wife. The Bible writers speak of a special type of sensual love that is only to be enjoyed by married couples, not for courting couples. There is another reason why couples should not get physically intimate until marriage that relates to the biological function of the sexual organs. We will look at this verse again in the last chapter to understand this other reason. When you get physical you ruin the purpose of courtship—finding out whether the two of you are compatible—and you become attached in a way that is not pleasing to God.

Because of the bond that forms between two people when they show physical affection towards each other, it is necessary to first make a commitment to that person that they will be the only person that you will ever show this kind of love to and that you will continually show it to them for as long as you both live. The results of breaking that bond causes hurt, especially on the side of the lady. This is partly why girls cry when they have been dumped by a guy whom they have kissed. A bond has formed between them because of their physical intimacy. When they break up the bond is torn and it hurts, especially on the side of the girl because of her unique emotional nature. No person who has made this bond with another person should ever have that bond broken. That is why God has placed it inside the covenant of marriage so that no one gets hurt by the breaking of that bond.

There is a reason why the minister officiating a wedding says "You may NOW kiss the bride." The idea is that until you are married you are not supposed to be kissing. The kiss on your wedding day should be your first kiss. Today the minister says this phrase more out of formality than out of the true meaning of the phrase. Getting to know your partner on a physical level is to be inside of a marriage covenant.

Showing sexual affection before marriage makes it easier to commit adultery. If you get physically intimate with the person you are courting, basically you showed sexual affection to someone without making a commitment to that person that they will be the only person that you will ever show sexual affection to. Thus, if you are showing sexual affection to someone that you are not married to while you are still single, you are more likely to show sexual affection to someone you are not married to when you are married. It's the same thing: showing sexual affection outside the commitment of marriage.

Showing physical affection before marriage also takes something away from the trust that couples are to have for each other. If you get physical before marriage, a wife may wonder at times, "If he kissed me, or slept with me and we weren't married, is he kissing other women, or sleeping with other women other than me, his wife?" Alternatively, if you didn't get physical before marriage, a wife may rest assured, "He kept himself from kissing me before we were married, so I know that he is strong enough to resist kissing other girls." She knows that she can trust you when you are away from home.

Spend more time in each other's homes than any other place. Get to know each other during the daytime, when there are adults nearby and when you will have the least temptation to fall into sin.

> The habit of sitting up late at night is customary, but it is not pleasing to God, even if you are both Christians. These untimely hours injure health, unfit the mind for the next day's duties, and have an appearance of evil. My brother, I hope you will have self-respect enough to shun this form of courtship. If you have an eye single to the glory of God, you will move with deliberate caution. You will not suffer lovesick sentimentalism to so blind your vision that you cannot discern the high claims that God has upon you as a Christian.
>
> *Messages to Young People* pg. 438

One thing that has made it easier for young men and women to fall into the sin of fornication is the desire to leave home as soon as they are financially able to do so. It is not necessary to be in a hurry to leave home. God does not require you to leave your parents' home once you get a job. As far as possible, remain with your parents; support the household with your time, money and strength. It is the home that prepares you to have a home of your own. You do not have to live on your own to be prepared for having a home of your own.

> It is by faithfulness to duty in the parental home that the youth are to prepare themselves for homes of their own.
>
> *Patriarchs and Prophets* pg. 176

Staying at home will allow you and the person that you are courting to have a more effective courtship; there will be little temptation to get physical and you will get to know each other's families, and they will get to know you. Family activities can be easily arranged, and these are encouraged.

This allows the two families to get better acquainted with each other as well as with the young man or young lady whom their daughter or son may one day marry. It makes for a much happier marriage experience if everyone knows each other well.

Easy on the Romance

When we speak of romance we speak of expressions of your emotional attraction to a particular person. This may be in the form of special gifts, singing songs, writing poems, saying "I love you" and other sentimental things, and so on. The books, movies and songs that we are exposed to have deceived us into believing that the time before marriage is a time for endless romance and physical affection, and that we should decide on whether or not to marry a person based on our romantic feelings for that person. But romance is not entirely necessary during courtship. Excessive expressions of your emotional attraction also work against the purpose of courtship: finding out whether or not you are compatible.

When two people act romantically towards each other they also form a bond. They develop strong feelings for each other and it becomes harder and harder to think clearly. Do not be in a rush to demonstrate your love towards someone. Let the relationship develop based on compatibility in life-work, in personality, in character and in terms of spiritual condition. Expressions of attraction may add to the flavour of the relationship, but never let it be the main ingredient. We need to refine our understanding of the place of these expressions in courtship. We need to stop watching the love stories in movies and we need to stop reading about them in novels. Satan is deceiving us and it is ruining our families.

> The course many parents pursue in allowing their children to be indolent and to gratify a desire for reading romance, is unfitting them for real life. Novel and story-book reading is the greatest evil that youth can indulge in. Novel and love-story readers always fail to make good practical mothers. They live in an unreal world. They are air-castle builders, living in an imaginary world. They become sentimental, and have sick fancies. Their artificial life spoils them for anything useful. They are dwarfed in intellect, although they flatter themselves that they are superior in mind and manners. Exercise in household labor will be of the greatest advantage to young girls.
>
> *Christian Education* pg. 17

In the youthful mind marriage is clothed with romance, and it is difficult to divest it of this feature, with which imagination covers it, and to impress the mind with a sense of the weighty responsibilities involved in the marriage vow. This vow links the destinies of the two individuals with bonds which naught but the hand of death should sever. Every marriage engagement should be carefully considered, for marriage is a step taken for life. Both the man and the woman should carefully consider whether they can cleave to each other through the vicissitudes of life as long as they both shall live.

The Adventist Home pg. 340

A godly husband will know that it is his duty to show physical affection to his wife, to tell her that he loves her, to show thoughtfulness and kindness, and to give her gifts. And so it is with the wife. These things are a given once you are married. You should not decide on whether or not to marry a person based on how romantic they are, or how much physical affection they show. Your decision should be based on character and the other compatibility considerations mentioned previously. For this reason, romance and physical affection are not needed while courting. In fact, they make it harder for you to decide whether or not you are compatible with the person you are with.

I once had a conversation with a very dear pastor friend of mine. At the time he was doing his master's in theology. He was much older than me and already married. I asked him about how he met his wife and how they got to the point of getting married. During the time of courtship they had not shown any physical affection or romance to each other whatsoever. Their courtship was exactly what a courtship should be: a time to evaluate compatibility for marriage.

He shared something interesting with me. After a few years of marriage he had a conversation with his wife and he told her that during the courtship days he did not know if when they were married that he would ever even be able to hold her hand. After 10 years of marriage and 2 children later, he was glad that they did it that way. The wait was worth it.

Not showing physical affection and expressions of your love before marriage is no evidence that it will be like that during marriage. Let courtship be the evaluation time that it is supposed to be and let the expressions of love come later.

True love is a high and holy principle, altogether different in character from that love which is awakened by impulse and which suddenly dies when severely tested. It is by faithfulness to duty in the parental home that the youth are to prepare themselves for homes of their own. Let them here practice self-denial and manifest kindness, courtesy, and Christian sympathy. Thus love will be kept warm in the heart, and he who goes out from such a household to stand at the head of a family of his own will know how to promote the happiness of her whom he has chosen as a companion for life. Marriage, instead of being the end of love, will be only its beginning.

Patriarchs and Prophets pg. 176

Character is built in the home. The person whom you marry will have the greatest effect on your character development than every other person on earth. When you make the decision for someone to marry, you should do everything to ensure that you are thinking clearly. Romance and physical affection dull your ability to make a rational decision. Leave this out during courtship, you don't need it. Let marriage be the beginning of love.

More Counselling
Counselling should not stop once you are courting. You still need to speak to your team of supporters while you are courting, and you still need to spend a lot of time in prayer. Now that you are courting, you also have the opportunity to meet more people who know the person you are courting well. You can ask them about the person's character, background, personality and so on. It is a great time to get to know the family you may one day be getting married into.

Let the woman who desires a peaceful, happy union, who would escape future misery and sorrow, inquire before she yields her affections, Has my lover a mother? What is the stamp of her character? Does he recognize his obligations to her? Is he mindful of her wishes and happiness? If he does not respect and honor his mother, will he manifest respect and love, kindness and attention, toward his wife? When the novelty of marriage is over, will he love me still? Will he be patient with my mistakes, or will he

Whether your courtship ends in engagement or whether it ends by you going separate ways, your courtship has been successful.

be critical, overbearing, and dictatorial? True affection will overlook many mistakes; love will not discern them.

Messages to Young People pg. 450

If there ever was a subject that needed to be viewed from every standpoint, it is this. The aid of the experience of others, and a calm, careful weighing of the matter on both sides, is positively essential. It is a subject that is treated altogether too lightly by the great majority of people. Take God and your God-fearing parents into your counsel, young friends. Pray over the matter. Weigh every sentiment, and watch every development of character in the one with whom you think to link your life destiny. The step you are about to take is one of the most important in your life, and should not be taken hastily. While you may love, do not love blindly.

The Review and Herald, January 26, 1886

Ending It

As you get to know the person that you are courting, more about that person's character, personality and spirituality will be revealed to you and yours to them. There will be a lot of things that you did not know about them before you started courtship. With this new information you may realize that you will not be compatible for marriage. There is nothing wrong with this. This was the purpose of courtship—to determine compatibility for marriage. End the courtship if you realize that you are not compatible. You can discuss this even with the person that you are courting and you can decide to end the courtship. This is not something that you should decide on overnight. Think it through, discuss it with your parents, and then make a decision.

If children would be more familiar with their parents, if they would confide in them, and unburden to them their joys and sorrows, they would save themselves many a future heartache. When perplexed to know what course is right, let them lay the matter just as they view it before their parents, and ask advice of them. Who are so well calculated to point out their dangers as godly parents? Who can understand their peculiar temperaments so well as they?

Messages to Young People pg. 450-451

Whether your courtship ends in engagement or whether it ends by you going separate ways, your courtship has been successful. As long as you did not get involved too deeply emotionally by romance and physical affection, ending your courtship will not cause a lot of heartache. There may be disappointment, there may be a sense of loss, but you are far better off in this case than if you were following the dating procedure.

It is romance and physical affection that dating allows for that makes ending a courtship more difficult. Couples get into a situation where they feel like they don't want to lose the person that they are with. And so you have a bond with someone that has little to do with your compatibility for marriage and has everything to do with your romantic feelings. If you avoid the romance and the physical affection, if you keep the focus of the relationship on a getting-to-know-each-other basis, ending the courtship is much easier.

Be careful also of jumping from one courtship to the next searching for "the perfect one." There are no perfect people. You are not perfect either. And in jumping from one person to the next you may hurt a lot of feelings. Spend time in prayer and consultation with your team of supporters. Let God lead you. Keep two ideas always in balance: one, you are not married and this is an evaluation period, and two, you are dealing with the feelings, hopes and dreams of another human being and you have the potential to cause a lot of hurt. Guard your emotions and affections. Remember that, until you are married, the person whom you are courting may also at any time come to the conclusion that you are not suited for each other and end the courtship. Be careful of bonding too deeply.

If you come to the conclusion during courtship that you are compatible with the person that you are courting, you may decide to get married. A couple may decide together, in discussion, that they should get married. Usually, it is the young man who proposes to the young lady and she decides whether or not to accept the request. Engagement and the wedding are the subjects of next chapter. We will also look at one vital component of marriage: service to each other's needs.

But I've Already Gone Too Far
When we come to God we do not come with perfect lives, having never done anything bad; we come with broken lives, lives with mistakes, and imperfections. Jesus did not come to call righteous people to be a part of His kingdom; He came to call sinners to repentance. The fact that you may

have gone beyond what God calls holy, righteous and good in the area of courtship does not mean that your case is a lost case. Jesus is there to cleanse you from your sin, to wash you, to make you clean and to give you the strength of character to do what is right in His eyes.

If we confess our sins, he is faithful and just to forgive us our sins, and to cleanse us from all unrighteousness.

1 John 1:9

God takes our lives, washes away our sin and He makes us new people.

Therefore if any man be in Christ, he is a new creature: old things are passed away; behold, all things are become new.

1 Corinthians 5:17

Come to God, confess your sins, and seek to do what is right. The past does not matter. Make a decision that from this day onwards you will do what is right.

He that covereth his sins shall not prosper: but whoso confesseth and forsaketh them shall have mercy.

Proverbs 28:13

Summary

Courtship is a time to get to know each other. A lot of time should be spent in one-on-one conversation with the person that you are courting. Physical affection and excessive romance are to be avoided. This is a time to determine compatibility in terms of personality, character and spirituality. Physical affection and excessive romance at this stage may lead to infatuation and will make it difficult to end the courtship if couples realize that they are not compatible. Counselling with parents, loved ones and spiritual mentors should continue.

Get to know the family of the person you are courting. Spend a lot of time at each other's homes. Family activities are encouraged. This allows the two families to get better acquainted with each other as well as with the young man or young lady who their daughter or son may one day marry. If you know that there is a possibility that you might be alone, get a family member or other responsible person to be present to ensure that you do not have the temptation to get physically affectionate.

Courtship is a time to find out whether or not you and the person that you are courting are compatible for marriage. If you find out that you are not, it is fine to end the courtship. Discuss the incompatibility with the person that you are courting, and, if need be, also with the person's parents. Avoiding physical affection and romance during courtship will make ending the courtship much easier.

Chapter Five

On Your Knee

"For even the Son of man came not to be ministered unto, but to minister, and to give his life a ransom for many."

Mark 10:45

On Your Knee

Usually when a man proposes marriage to a woman he gets on one knee. This practice is not something that is required; however it does demonstrate the beautiful truth of what marriage is all about: service. In this chapter we will look at some of the aspects with regards to the marriage proposal and the wedding.

The Marriage Proposal

David had the intention of courting Lia. David and Lia did not court, yet David's experience in seeking God's will during those days taught him something about marriage. We are told from Inspiration that we ought to spend twice as much time in prayer when we anticipate a step towards marriage. David was doing exactly that when he wanted to know whether or not God wanted him to court Lia.

During that time in his life David was really doing well spiritually, financially, emotionally and in all other aspects of life. He was living the life that I mentioned in Chapter 1, a life of being content as a single person. David enjoyed being single so much that the thought of getting into a courting relationship scared him a bit. He wanted to stay single for much longer and enjoy the benefits of being single: the free time, the personal development, the freedom. However, he had in the back of his mind that he would like to get married one day. Just not now.

David believed that God had brought Lia into his life to show him the blessings of marriage, the blessings of having someone to be there with you if you fall, to share your life with, and to help you to be a more responsible person. Lia was spiritually on point, so there was no issue there. In fact, he had struggled to find in other girls the same spiritual maturity that he had seen in Lia. His only issue was that he didn't want to get married. He was enjoying the single life.

I wish this for every young person: that you will so enjoy being single that you will have to think it over, and pray earnestly before you step into a one-on-one relationship. But, back to the story. As I mentioned, David was praying a lot each day, asking God what He wanted for his life. One afternoon, while praying, David said to God, "Lord, I don't need a woman in my life right now." In that prayer, God spoke to David in His own special way and asked him the question "What about what *she* needs?"

Through all his prayers, David was only considering what he wanted and what he needed. He was only considering what would make him happy and what would give him success in life. Here was God now saying to him, "You missed the point." Never did he consider that Lia might need a man in her life. Never did he consider that she might want someone in her life. David began to look at things in a different perspective, and realised the true purpose of marriage: service.

> In your life union your affections are to be tributary to each other's happiness. Each is to minister to the happiness of the other. This is the will of God concerning you.
>
> *Messages to Young People* pg. 451

Marriage is about service. It is not about my happiness alone. It is about making sure that the person that I married to is also happy. Marriage is not just about what you can do for me; it is more about what I can do for you. So, when the young man gets on his knee, and asks the young lady "Will you marry me?" he is saying "Can I be your servant for the rest of my life?"

> Husbands, love your wives, even as Christ also loved the church, and gave himself for it.
>
> Ephesians 5:25

How did Christ love the church? By giving Himself for her; by choosing death rather than to see the church lost. Loving means giving yourself; it means placing what my wife or husband wants and needs ahead of what I want and need. We are to love each other as we love ourselves.

With this concept of service in mind, it is also important, once again, to ensure that you are well-mated. The home of a married couple is a place to rest and to recuperate from being in the battlefield with Satan in the world. The home is the place where you minister to your spouse's needs and your spouse ministers to your needs, so that you both can be ready again to take on the attacks of Satan.

The home is not a mission field. It is a base camp. It is a place where you can let down your guard and rest a bit. If you are not on the same spiritual level as the person you are married to, the home becomes a mission field as well, and thus, a place where you are vulnerable to the attacks of Satan. Be careful who you marry. Marry someone whom you can minister to, but also someone who can minister to you.

Do not enter into an engagement unless you are sure that your relationship is one that God approves of. Engagement is a promise to marry. You should never enter into an engagement unless you are sure that you should marry this person. It is a sin to go back on this promise to marry. However, if you realise during your engagement that you are not compatible, or that you will be going against God's will by marrying the person, end the engagement.

You may say, "But I have given my promise, and shall I now retract it?" I answer, If you have made a promise contrary to the Scriptures, by all means retract it without delay, and in humility before God repent of the infatuation that led you to make so rash a pledge. Far better take back such a promise, in the fear of God, than keep it, and thereby dishonor your Maker.

Messages to Young People pg. 441

The Wedding

I think that it is in order to say a few things with regards to the wedding ceremony. God enjoys marriages, it was His idea. Jesus performed His first miracle at a marriage celebration. It is a joyous occasion when two people commit themselves to each other in a manner that God ordained.

It is unfortunate, though, that over the years wedding ceremonies have become more about display and extravagance than about an earnest desire to please and honour God. It is unfortunate that they have become a place to indulge in things that God forbids. We must remember that God attends our weddings. He is the most honoured guest and we should have a wedding ceremony that will be pleasing to Him more than to any human being attending the ceremony and celebration.

Worldliness has taken over our concept of what a wedding ceremony and celebration should look like. The worldly music that is played at a wedding celebration, the dancing, the wearing of cosmetics and jewellery, all these things go against the principles of the church of God. We need to put these away and seek only to please God at our weddings. Couples go to a great expense to have extravagant wedding ceremonies and use money that would have better been used in establishing a wholesome Christian home on unnecessary ornaments and accessories:

> Marriage ceremonies are made matters of display, extravagance, and self-indulgence. But if the contracting parties are agreed in religious belief and practice, and everything is consistent, and the ceremony be conducted without display and extravagance, marriage at this time need not be displeasing to God. There is no reason why we should make great parade or display, even if the parties were perfectly suited to each other. It has always seemed so very inappropriate to me to see the marriage ordinance associated with hilarity and glee and a pretense of something. No. It is an ordinance ordained of God, to be looked upon with the greatest solemnity. As the family relation is formed here below, it is to give a demonstration of what they shall be, the family in heaven above. The glory of God is ever to be made first.
>
> *The Adventist Home* pg. 100-101

Wearing wedding rings and engagement rings has become more prevalent over the years. This is not how we started out. There is no instruction from the Bible that we should wear rings as symbols of marriage or to tell other people that we are married or engaged. Wearing of rings, in any form, goes against God's principles of modesty and simplicity in the way we dress ourselves. Instead, God wants us to show that we are married by the way that we behave around other people.

> Whose adorning let it not be that outward adorning of plaiting the hair, and of wearing of gold, or of putting on of apparel; but let it be the hidden man of the heart, in that which is not corruptible, even the ornament of a meek and quiet spirit, which is in the sight of God of great price. For after this manner in the old time the holy women also, who trusted in God, adorned themselves, being in subjection unto their own husbands.
>
> 1 Peter 3:3-5

Here the Lord, through his apostle, speaks expressly against the wearing of gold. Let those who have had experience see to it that they do not lead others astray on this point by their example. That ring encircling your finger may be very plain, but it is useless, and the wearing of it has a wrong influence upon others.

The Review and Herald July 8, 1880

We need not wear the sign, for we are not untrue to our marriage vow, and the wearing of the ring would be no evidence that we were true. I feel deeply over this leavening process which seems to be going on among us, in the conformity to custom and fashion. Not one penny should be spent for a circlet of gold to testify that we are married.

Testimonies to Ministers and Gospel Workers pg. 180-181

Do not feel that you need to impress the family, friends and neighbours with extravagance and display. Seek only to please God.

Blessed Fountain

In the previous chapter I mentioned that we would look at another reason why physical affection such as kissing, holding and fondling, is not appropriate before marriage. Remembering the concept of service, let's look at the verse again from the book of Proverbs:

Let thy fountain be blessed: and rejoice with the wife of thy youth. Let her be as the loving hind and pleasant roe; let her breasts satisfy thee at all times; and be thou ravished always with her love.

Proverbs 5:18-19

In this verse Solomon is demonstrating something that he knows about the human body that is not easy to notice. A woman is not as easily sexually aroused as a man is. A man may just see a naked woman and in less than 10 seconds he is physically ready to have sex. It is not the same with women. A woman needs to be spoken to in a loving manner, touched, caressed, and kissed a lot before she is physically ready to have sex. This behaviour is called "petting", "foreplay", or "love-making".

As a woman hears love-talk from her husband, as she is touched, caressed, kissed and as her breasts are being fondled by him, her body reacts by becoming ready for sexual intercourse. It takes a much, much longer time for a woman to become aroused and prepared for sexual intercourse than it does for a man.

Unless there is foreplay, or love-making, a woman will not be physically ready for intercourse and her husband can cause damage to her sexual organs if he proceeds without her being ready. This is the same damage that occurs when a woman is raped. Her sexual organs were not prepared by love-making and so they are damaged. In essence then, if there is not enough love-making before intercourse, a man can physically rape his wife. She may dislike having sex for the rest of the marriage.

This then is the second important reason why kissing and petting should not be done before marriage. If a couple participated in kissing and petting before marriage there is a tendency to skip over this important part of sex, or to keep it short, when they are married. If there has not been sufficient foreplay, the woman is thus not prepared for intercourse and her husband can cause a lot of physical damage to her. Foreplay is a part of sex, because without it, sex would be painful to a woman. Thus, if you engage in foreplay before marriage you are engaging in the sexual act and thus committing fornication. Read that sentence again.

Solomon is also describing this act of foreplay in the context of marriage; the behaviour that he is describing belongs to married couples only, not to courting couples. Nowhere in scripture will you find foreplay being recommended for unmarried people. If you are engaging in foreplay while courting, I urge you to stop. Save it for marriage.

Couples should have sex education before getting married. As human beings we always need to be educated. We do not know how to do things naturally; we need to be taught how to talk, how to read, how to dress ourselves, and so on. All through life we need to be taught. The same is true with sex. We need to be taught how to have sex, before getting married, on a theoretical basis. Not now, but shortly before marriage, get sex education with your future spouse. There are brilliant books on the subject by Christian authors. Also, many pastors, together with their wives, include this in their marriage counselling program.

I've Really Gone Too Far
The Bible tells a beautiful story about what God thinks of sinners. In the book of John, we have there recorded the story of the woman who was

caught in adultery. Jesus went against what everyone one would have expected of a righteous person. Here was a Man who was pure and holy, who had committed no sin, who, amongst all the people that were gathered there, was the only one worthy to stone her to death. Yet His words to her were "Neither do I condemn you. Go and sin no more."

The Bible does not paint Jesus as a condemning dictator who wants nothing less than perfection from us. Instead, Jesus is shown to be the forgiving Saviour of sinners who pardons our sins, dies in our place, and covers our lives with His life. Jesus is shown to be the friend of sinners and while we spend time with Him, we are changed and become like Him in character.

You have not gone too far to the point that God is able to forgive you and to cleanse you from your sins. If you feel that your life has been a mess, come to God, repent of your sins, turn away from them and seek strength from God. And if you fall again, remember, He is already there to hear your prayer and forgive you again. Keep getting back up!

> My little children, these things write I unto you, that ye sin not. And if any man sin, we have an advocate with the Father, Jesus Christ the righteous.
>
> 1 John 2:1

Summary

Marriage is about service; it is about meeting the needs of the person that you are married to so that you both may be better prepared to take on the challenges of living a Christian life. You should only enter into an engagement if you are sure that the person you are courting will be a suitable life-partner for you and you for them.

Weddings should be simple and modest. They should be pleasing to God before being pleasing to friends and family. Wedding rings are not needed. A couple should also be well educated when it comes to sex. Foreplay is an important part of sex. Couples that engage in foreplay before marriage are committing fornication. Foreplay should be left for marriage.

A Final Word

Where are you when it comes to relationships? Are you a young lady who's been hurt by a young man? Perhaps you're a young man who has hurt a young lady and you are looking for way of getting into a relationship without the risk of hurting another girl. Maybe this is the first time that you have come across the courtship procedure and God's courtship principles and you didn't know how bad the dating procedure actually is. Wherever you are, my prayer for you is that you will deeply consider going about relationships God's way.

Decide today that you will not do relationships the way the world does relationships. The dating procedure has caused a lot of hurt; it is a method of doing relationships that goes against the principles of God's kingdom. It is filled with deception, lust, fornication and all the principles of Satan's kingdom. It is not God's method for you to become ready for marriage; it is Satan's method for you to prepare for your divorce.

Do relationships God's way! You don't have to learn how to flirt, you don't have to learn how to play hard to get. It's not necessary for you to become a ladies-man. It is not necessary for you to become the talk of all the boys. It's not necessary for you to learn any pick-up lines. All you need to learn is to be a citizen of God's kingdom; to seek first the kingdom of God and His righteousness, and all these other things will be added unto you.

How great would it be if there was a love revolution in the world and in the church? A reformation in the area of relationships? How great would it be if young people completed their education, established themselves financially, emotionally and spiritually, courted someone and then got married God's way? We would have better homes, better families, better churches, and better communities. In Isaiah God calls His people to be the repairers of the breach, to fix the brokenness that Satan has caused in the world. Also, through Jeremiah we are given this admonition:

> Thus saith the LORD, Stand ye in the ways, and see, and ask for the old paths, where is the good way, and walk therein, and ye shall find rest for your souls.
>
> Jeremiah 6:16

In the courtship procedure we have an old path, old principles, a good way. It is up to us to decide whether or not to walk therein. The people that God was speaking to in Jeremiah 6:16 said "We will not walk therein." How is it with you? Will you decide to walk in these old paths, the good way? The promise is that "You will find rest for your soul."

Remember that you are not choosing between following a procedure and not following a procedure; you are choosing which procedure to follow: God's procedure, or Satan's procedure. I invite you to be a part of the revolution. It starts with you. Decide to do it God's way, and follow through. Let there be a revolution. Let's do it God's way!

References and Resources

Adventist Family Ministries. *Divorce and Remarriage in the Seventh-day Adventist Church: What the Divorce Statistics Say*. Online. Available at: http://family.adventist.org/home---divorce-and-remarriage-in-the-seventh-day-adventist-church.html [Accessed 19 January 2015].

AudioVerse. www.audioverse.org. This is a great resource that every Adventist should use on a regular basis. There are many brilliant talks on courtship available on this website. Search for talks by Alan and Nicole Parker, Phil Mills and Jorge Baute.

Brian Schwertley. *The Christian Family*, ch. 7: *Dating Versus Biblical Courtship*. Online. Available at: http://www.reformedonline.com/uploads/1/5/0/3/15030584/chapter_7_christian_family.pdf [Accessed 19 January 2015].

Deanna L.M. Johnston. *How Courting a Man Ruined Me*. Online. Available at: http://www.deannawriter.com/how-courting-a-man-ruined-me/ [Accessed 19 January 2015]. I've also shared it on Evernote: http://tiny.cc/uwocpx

Eric & Leslie Ludy. *When God writes your love story*. Winston and Brooks, Inc. 2004.

Henry Wright. *The Holy Spirit & Choosing a Mate*. Community Praise Center. 2009. Audio file. Available at: http://www.cpcsda.org/pages/page.asp?page_id=160784&seriesId=16617 [Accessed 19 January 2015].

Jeffrey Brown. *Single and Gifted*. Autumn House. 2002.

Jere Franklin. *God's Appointed*. Remnant Publications. 2008.

Joshua Harris. *Boy Meets Girl: Say hello to courtship*. Multnomah Books. 2005.

Ravi Zacharias. *I, Isaac, Take Thee, Rebekah: Moving from Romance to Lasting Love*. Thomas Nelson, Inc. 2005.

Sharon L. Phillips, Richard D. Phillips. *Holding Hands, Holding Hearts: Recovering a Biblical View of Christian Dating*. P&R Publishing Company. 2006.

Notes

Notes

Notes

www.ingramcontent.com/pod-product-compliance
Lightning Source LLC
Chambersburg PA
CBHW060124050426
42448CB00010B/2018